BOC

LETTERS FROM A DIFFERENT LAND

by

Boo Lundy

Benbow Publications

Published in 2018 by Benbow Publications.

British Library
Cataloguing in Publication Data

ISBN: 9781908760395

First Edition

ACKNOWLEDGEMENTS

I wish to gratefully acknowledge all the help and guidance I have received in compiling this book; with particular thanks to Isaiah Abbotsbury and his guide.

Thanks also to Lucy Harpur, who edited and formatted this book, and to Sue Gresham, who paginated the work and to my close friend Skylark who transcribed all of the writings within this book.

Without these patient people this book would not have been possible.

Boo Lundy

In memory of my mum and dad, grandmas and grandpas, aunts, uncles, and cousins.

INTRODUCTION

Skylark is a Christian Spiritualist, with a lifelong love of history and the Christian faith. This developed into an interest in the symbolism contained in the Bible, and the teachings of Judaism, and is growing to incorporate other world faiths.

The name *Skylark* is symbolic of her love of the birds and nature in general. *Skylark* is also a clairsentient medium, who has written with her guides and inspirers for many years. She began to gradually notice the communication was deviating from her usual sources into well-known names, which would be recognised today.

After talking with her friend and mentor, Isaiah Abbotsbury, it was decided to publish the communications/letters in the form of a book, with the great assistance of Boo Lundy. The first draft commenced on the 3rd August, 2015, at 14:28.

'Letters from a Different Land' is the end result, and is *Skylark's* first published book.

CONTENTS

A list of contents in alphabetical order, including dates and times of channeling, can be found at the end of this book.

A GUIDE CALLED RACHEL

KARMA
(19/07/17 - 08:18)

To begin with, none of us were going to explain about karma. It was thought a good idea to let the communicators speak for themselves, and naturally karma was bound to pop up. The suggestion was that this would promote discussion... and that wouldn't be a bad thing. However, after *Skylark* discussed the idea of karma with her friend Isaiah Abbotsbury, it was decided to begin with the subject.

I am the guide *Skylark* considered asking to do this, and then she thought about her doorkeeper Matthias. Both of us are evolved souls, and we can easily explain karma to you. As Matthias is going to communicate a letter, later on, it was agreed that I would be the one to do the explaining.

Karma is a deep subject, on many different levels, and perhaps too much to give at once... I have decided to keep it simple. That will be enough to give you an idea, and maybe a few questions will result as a consequence. If you live near a spiritualist church or have a friend on their spiritual pathway, they might be able to help you with this. For those of you already established on your pathway, you know what to do... but of course, manage your link in the process in the correct manner. I have to say this as *Skylark* is keen on the correct way to link with your guides and spirit in general. So, I am doing what she feels is correct... as *Skylark* is in charge of this piece, not I. If I write something she isn't sure of, she will challenge me and speak to Isaiah about it. 'Good girl' is what I say back to her. 'That's the way to do it' as they say!

So, what is karma? Very simply put, it is *'you reap what you sow,'* or *'do as you would be done by'* is another well-known saying. Another that many of you know is *'what goes around comes around.'* Each action that we take has a consequence, and this consequence is part of the law of karma. So, when we go to work each day and are grumpy or rude to our colleagues, it has a karmic consequence. If a nation bombs another, that has a *'what goes around comes around'* process for each individual involved. People may die as a consequence, and to take a life is a grave act indeed. Each person who is grumpy or rude to their work colleagues will have to understand what that feels like. Now, perhaps someone has joined the army, or has been forced into a military organisation against their will, which can happen in times of conflict... all of this is taken into consideration. If, perhaps, a person is part of a worldwide or national terrorist organisation, and has joined because they wish to... that is a different thing altogether. If you are an individual with hate in your heart and destruction on your mind, again the severity of your actions will have a just result with your karma.

You see karma is impartial... completely impartial! This means that it responds according to what has happened. Now, if it is goodness of heart that has been uppermost in the life of a man or woman, that has the corresponding karma.

It has been on the news recently, in the United Kingdom, about acid attacks against individuals, and the same thing is happening to women around the world. Mark my words all of you, as this will have an impact on your karma, if you are behaving in such a manner... you will have to understand what you have done at some stage of your life! It may be a karmic response in this life, or another, but either way it cannot be avoided.

How are the people of this Earth going to understand that thoughts, words, and deeds have consequences, if these are not felt, and deeply so? Karma is such a just and impartial process. It is also unconnected to God. God does not judge! Never have I witnessed him judge another individual. It is the way we live that 'judges us,' and not any judgement, or weighing of the scales of life, in the spirit plane. You reap as you sow, simple as that. Now I have got that over with, I will say a little about the communicators. There is more - of course there is - as there is the karma we have agreed to as part of our life now... but that is enough to begin with.

It is in the karma of every individual, in this book of letters, to speak to you all. It can be for a variety of reasons. Perhaps their past lives were one of goodness and service. Maybe, even they have learnt from their karma, and are working hard trying to understand more, and have enthusiasm for each new life on the Earth, which has been offered to them. *Skylark* has requested one or two communicators out of interest. This has been heard by us, and will be fulfilled because of her karma. She has a love of history, so one of these individuals to speak will be Augustus, Emperor of Rome.

He is one of the many who has learnt and is now a more peaceful soul. The characteristics he possessed as emperor, he no longer has, and the lives since lived have taught him humility and a lot else. It wasn't easy at first, as he still thought he could bark orders out in the spirit plane, and he tried to. So, he had to be segregated, and remained so, until he was considered safe to be with other people. We couldn't allow him to think he was able to exert control and order executions. He had to see, feel, and learn what his life had done to others, and what his karma gave back to him. I am sure you can begin to understand why it wasn't easy for him at the start. Still, he was shown a lot more respect than what he ever gave. This same respect is given to all who gravitate towards the lower levels of the spirit plane, as Augustus did. He is now a reformed man and uses a different name: he will talk to you about his experiences. *Skylark's* doorkeeper Matthias will be standing close by, as he will with all the communicators.

One will be a well-known name, who has helped the people of the world a great deal. He is also considered to be an archangel, and his name is Gabriel… he is a shining example of goodness and love. You will also be hearing from God, so expect a revelation or two from him. The contents of this book have been considered providently, to bring you goodness and variety, experience and an inclination to experience more, so I hope you enjoy it. If you do have any questions, ask around, seek the reply, and hopefully you may have more as a consequence.

With blessings to you all,
Rachel

WINSTON CHURCHILL

DID I MAKE A DIFFERENCE?
(15/06/17 - 10:56)

I was lonely as a child, and felt that I mattered little. Now, if you knew who I was, you wouldn't believe it… although who we are in spirit makes no difference. It is what we say and do that means the most, and I have said and done a lot of things that I am not always proud of. I have had to answer for them here, where I am now; in the most heavenly of places. I have also had thanks from people too. So, perhaps I am not as curmudgeonly as I appeared to be when I was in government.

Winston Churchill is one of the names I am known by, as titles have no use or any meaning in heaven… or 'spirit' as it is often called. I decline to use mine and all of my friends do. You may call me what you wish and 'black dog' will do, although I no longer suffer that affliction. It is in my past, along with a lot of things. I no longer feel that I do not matter, because of my history. I have learnt a lot, which means that I can be of service to others, and the country I still love.

Perhaps you scoff and think it impossible… 'so be it,' if that's how you feel. I don't have to prove anything to anybody. I also answer to no-one, as God does not expect me to bow down before him, or follow the commands of any other individual; as none are ever given. It is so different to my life before, when I had to 'toe the party line', or smile at despots like Koba.

Stalin was dead to life… his eyes had no shine to them. I knew when I looked at him, that here was a man who would do anything for personal power. Did you know that he lingers in the lower levels of spirit, still thinking he can take a life with a smile, or the tilt of his head? Perhaps you don't, but he does, and he will remain there until he can see the error of his ways, and turn his face to the light of life eternal. It is not vengeance, as there is no such thing, unless you live on the Earth. There it is in abundance, but not here - never here - as we only grow to the good side of our nature, and not the Earth-bound one. Stalin still thinks he is the man who commands millions, and behaves thus. He will learn, just as all like him have to. Time is not of the essence, so no matter how long it takes him, or Adolf Hitler, for example, to face the truth of their lives, they will stay in the darkness of their soul.

I have had to face aspects of my life that I felt uncomfortable with, and did so willingly so I could learn, and help the man or woman I spoke to. I have talked to soldiers who died in Normandy and Jews who suffered in Auschwitz. I told them everything I knew, and hid nothing; as that would not help them or me on our path to redemption. I faced their anger at my replies, and my soul vibrated when I saw that the truth can heal. I am not the only person who has faced the karma of their life, as we all have to. It is inescapable, and a just way of dealing with the iniquities we have committed. None can walk away from their karma, unlike the justice of this world called Earth... there the mighty often do not fall. Here the mighty are seen by the light of their soul, and sometimes it is shocking. Love is never far away though, no matter what you have done, as God never gives up. He is so bright and positive, that even when he is insulted, all he ever gives in response is love.

Sometimes I thought he walked with me during the difficult days of my life, when I had troubling decisions to make. I now know he did, and he does not judge me, as he is not that kind of man. I judged myself when I looked back, and reflected on what I could have done differently.

I regret a lot of things, and the bombing of Pearl Harbour is one of them, because of the resultant devastation of Hiroshima and Nagasaki. When the people of these cities passed to spirit, a lot of bright, developed souls rushed to their aid; to help them heal and know where they were. As they were given help, so was every single person who died, no matter the side. This also applies to the victims of any terror organisation, in the history of the Earth. None can bomb, maim, or take a life in the way of terror, and think it is justified... because it never is!

So, I walk the Earth, to see how I can help a people that I still love and respect. I go to places I would rather not, to listen and observe, and see history unravelling. I am not the only one, but that is their story to tell. Just as I try to help in ways that denies none their freewill, so does God. I shall say nothing more on the subject, as it is for God to describe later on in book... and he will.

For now, I would like to end with this thought, that *our words and deeds are part of our personal evolution… our journey to the light, which resides in each of us. How we go about it is our individual responsibility, which cannot be denied when we reflect in spirit, on our last Earth incarnation.* It is food for thought, so I leave that with you.

With the greatest of respect,
Winston Churchill

TUTANKHAMUN

A MYSTERY SOLVED
(16/06/17 - 16:59)

I was poisoned! After numerous attempts on my life, it was finally ended with poison. A not so subtle conclusion to a very short reign, as the poison was not quick-acting. If it had been, I may never have eaten and drunk that evening. It took its time, and I died leaving the way ahead for another ambitious relative. My wife was part of the scheme to remove me from the throne, and she paid for it in more ways than one. They say you can choose your friends and not your family, and how right they are. I would never have chosen mine, if I had been given the choice… I was not, and so a son of the Aten (in whom I never believed), was bullied, belittled, chased by murderers, and surrounded by them. A pathetic individual if ever there was one!

My family all wanted a taste of the ultimate power, and they felt it lay where I sat. I personally could have done without it, but felt I had no choice. I could never have stepped away, as that would have been my death sentence, but I lived as though I had one. When I died I felt some relief, and free at last.

I am interested in Egypt, and like the Pharaoh Hatshepsut still think of them as my people, despite having reincarnated many times since. All of my lives taught me something because I asked for them to. Our past lives are just that, our past, and each new one we enter into is a different experience. So, I have left behind the Egypt I knew, and am interested in what she has become, and will become.

It was no coincidence that Howard Carter found what he was looking for. He was determined, and it was his destiny. What he did with his find is a different story, but I am happy enough; as it is my mortal remains and not my soul that has been endlessly examined and talked about. Perhaps I am famous, but it is the mask and not the man that has found fame… is that so unusual, what I say? Think about it, and you will realise what fame can do.

Now, when I have not reincarnated, I have many interests.

Technology is one of them, so I can say with some authority that there is still a lot more for you to discover. Your cars can be more environmentally friendly, computers can be safer, from the malware that sometimes infests them, and the Earth can be a much greener place to live in, if you care for her more. By that, I mean Africa. A place with resources in abundance, which has been scrambled over by greedy nations, yet suffers such poverty. It can become a verdant land, but never will if the Earth continues to walk its current path.

But, I will not lecture you on that, as I will end up boring you, and another is due to tell it how it is… not me. Technology interests me. I may sound like a geek, but if I lived now, I would want to try everything that is new. I think I would have every kind of car or computer I could, and I would definitely want to experience space travel. Yet, I can go anywhere with just a thought, so I have already walked on the moon and gazed at Mars and the Milky Way. I have such opportunities, and I am grateful to the man who gave them to me.

*****

NICHOLAS (the SECOND of that name)

ANOTHER REMAINS?
(20/06/17 - 11:05)

Rasputin... now, that was a man I should never have trusted. I was desperate - we both were... my wife and I - desperate for our son to live; so another would not take his place. The imperial family of Russia trusted a licentious and greedy man, for the sake of their dynastic tendencies. Neither Alex nor I liked the idea of our son being replaced and wanted to avoid it, no matter what the cost... a figure we could not have anticipated!

I am here at the request of *Skylark*. She studied Russian history at A-level, and has been interested in the subject ever since. You will experience another of her requests later on... Conan Doyle is the name he uses.

As for me... I feel enough has been written on the subject of my family and its downfall. I would like to tell you something though, that none of you have any awareness of... otherwise what is the point? Yet any can read what they wish in the Halls of Learning, in spirit. It is all there... nothing is spared for a keen historian.

1. We got on with our guards at the end. Yes, a surprise it may be. They began to see we were human, weighed down by our lives, in more ways than one... but, we were on relatively decent terms with them. They knew we would die, and so did I... it was still a surprise when it came. Even if you are expecting death, to look it in the eye was frightening.

2. I disliked my cousin in England; I thought he was a coward with no backbone. I told him so when we finally spoke together, in a meeting in spirit, proposed by his parents. I said 'no' at first, as I could not forgive him. I thought he had signed our death warrant, or as much as. So, I wanted nothing to do with him after he died. It is different now... I have said my piece and he has explained much to me. England and Russia are resolved

never to be apart again.

3.   I have forgiven the men who murdered my family. This act helped me more than you can ever realise. It has unburdened my soul and allowed me to feel free. Not easy at first, as you might think… I needed help from a skilled counsellor in the Halls of Rest, called Thomas. A man, to this day, I call my friend, and always will.

I have said enough, and maybe too much, for a man that liked his privacy. It says in scripture, that if you ask you will receive (*Matthew 7:7-11*). I received so much and I asked too much from my people. I would like now to ask their forgiveness for everything I did… the wars, the pogroms, and my own inability to rule with compassion. I have learnt that it is never too late to turn around and look at life differently, and I have. I have learnt that I can help and not hinder, and I send absent healing to Russia. I have learnt that forgiveness unburdens the soul of so much, and that compassion is a quality of God. He is not a God of oracles against nations, sin and obedience, but one of such love and compassion, that it inspires me to try even harder for my people. I love them. I can say this now with true feeling. I hope I have the honour of being of service to them one day, if our paths cross in spirit.

With the greatest of respect,
Nicholas

MARIE ANTOINETTE

A FRENCH QUEEN'S PERSPECTIVE
(27/06/17 - 15:42)

I want to make one thing clear from the very outset… I had more compassion than the famous 'let them eat cake' saying. Although, I was a silly, giddy girl, and I know that. A lot has been explained to me since I was guillotined in front of a baying crowd.

I can understand that France had to change, but into what? Afterwards, or should I say, when the blood lust had been satiated, France was still suffering. Now, I see her and her people differently, and I love them all… every single one of them. It makes no difference where they live around the world, because I see so clearly from spirit, that language and custom are of no consequence. It is the same for all of us who will write. We love the people we are in that incarnation of. Yet love is bigger and broader than that. Because I have also been British, I feel the same about the people of the United Kingdom, and wish only the best in life for them.

You see, love in spirit is like that. It has no borders or boundaries, because we have a greater understanding about the qualities of love. It is all around us, and that is the big difference. It is God who is our inspiration, and his team of guides and the angelic-like souls that populate all levels of the spirit plane. I will leave that to Gabriel to explain about, and he will, in ways that will make some of you sit up straight.

…But, down to my life. I didn't like the French court, as it was one of the most licentious places I had ever been. Sometimes I couldn't believe my eyes at what I witnessed. The court of the Sun King was nothing, at times, to what I saw. Still, we paid for it in the end. I too have a secret which you will read… but not yet. Not until *Skylark* is old and grey… and then you will read what I have already said. Perhaps I am teasing or trying to be enigmatic… who knows, and perhaps who cares? I know it might be a little vexing and maybe not worth the wait, but one day, a long time away, another version of this book will be published.

I will finish with more one thing… when I was executed, I am glad that mobile phones had not been invented. It was bad enough with the crowds jeering, and, to be frank, if the mobile phone had been around, who knows what would have happened. So, I am glad that technology wasn't advanced enough for this to be the case. An odd thing to end on, but I have seen many things recorded that shouldn't have been. Still, mobile phones can be useful, and it is freewill whether to have one or not, when I next reincarnate. So, my thoughts are just that… my choice to say what I will, and not a recommendation.

Until we meet again, with the best of wishes,
Marie Antoinette

BENJAMIN DISRAELI

A FEW WORDS FROM A MAN CALLED DISRAELI
(28/06/17 - 14:52)

She was alright if you showed respect… Her Majesty Queen Victoria that is. I gave her this, and we got along as well as we could have done. Victoria had her favourites… some of this has been written about, but not all that history can tell. Yet, what I have witnessed on the television I am pleased with, and that includes portrayals of me.

It was always important to me to tell the truth. We had spin in the Houses of Parliament back then and a lot more personal privacy, so the public did not find out as much as they do these days. Even now, things have slipped through the hands of journalists, without them understanding what they have. 'So be it,' is all I can say on that. The profession of journalism isn't my favourite. Nowadays, in my opinion, it is the story rather than the truth, which in some newspapers is the main thrust of matters. Well now, do not take *Skylark* to task about this, as I stress, it is my opinion and not hers. She doesn't read the newspapers, but enjoys the Andrew Marr show on the television… it is a favourite of mine too.

We all have our little secrets in life. It wouldn't be normal if we didn't, but it is what they are that matters. The fact that *Skylark* uses a nom de plume is important, as she doesn't wish for publicity. She would far rather write unhindered, and that is what all in spirit wish for. You see, 'notoriety' and 'publicity' are double-edged swords.

Tutankhamun is a friend of mine. His life has been endlessly catalogued, but what the man is like, none know. You now know that technology is a favourite of his, but you didn't before. He gave a little of the truth of his life now, to show you that we in heaven are as normal as you are. It doesn't make any of us wiser because we have passed on. What it can and often does is make us less judgemental, and I applaud this quality. It is difficult not to be judgemental when you live on the Earth. If your best friend is found out to be a fraudulent person, then you could be tarred with the same brush. Not so in heaven. It is the individual that is important and how they lived their life, not the idea that because they are friends with so-and-so then they must be like-minded.

It was a matter of great importance when I was in Parliament, that I tried my best, always. To get to the top of the greasy pole wasn't easy, and I say 'well done' to any that do achieve that. My maiden speech didn't go down at all well... because I was a Jew it made the other members of Parliament less tolerant of me... a quality that was not to their favour. I dislike inequality of any sort. I like the fact that *Skylark* is a Christian Spiritualist, yet she is interested in religion in general. She has immense respect for Judaism, and although she wouldn't walk that path, she enjoys the scriptures and tries to discover what they mean. This doesn't make her 'religious,' but interesting to me and one or two others. She also understands freewill - allowing me to speak in this way - and will decide later whether to edit it out, or not. Her friend, Isaiah Abbotsbury, will guide her on this, with God listening in, no doubt... their choice, not mine.

So, you can see how freewill is of paramount importance, and spin is afforded little. Can you bury a news item in another? 'Yes,' is the answer... but not if you read between the lines. So, I encourage all of you to do just that... read between the lines and see what else is on the page. I may not be popular for saying this, but I have noticed that little things go blindly by a lot of people, when they would be important to them.

We had spin in my day, along with anti-Semitism. I would like to say - no, will say - that pogroms are a disgusting period of history, in any country that experienced them. Sectarianism goes against the grain, and it is fear that lies at the back of it. Fear of the 'other,' and lack of knowledge of different cultures and practices. If you feel this is part of your character, then ask. As the Bible says, 'ask and it will be given.' Knock on the door of a synagogue and seek information. Go to your Muslim brothers and sisters, and find out about Islam and their culture. Jewish and Muslim people are flesh and blood, like everyone else. The only variation is that, the path they walk to salvation is a little different. Does that matter? No, if I am honest, it does not. So, rather than lash out, find out... and it will make a difference to your life and theirs.

*****

14

JESUS CHRIST

A SON OF ISRAEL
(29/06/17 - 15:40)

My life isn't as straight forward as you may think. I am an immensely busy person; so is God and a whole host of other angelic-like souls. I say 'angelic-like' because angels are a story in themselves. As my twin soul, Gabriel, is considered to be an archangel, he will be the best person to tell you most about them… or not, as may be the case.

My life in the scriptures was one of beauty. Never mind how I was *supposed* to die, and note I say 'supposed' as even that involves a lot of explanation. So, perhaps I had better tell it to you straight, as I am that kind of man… *I was not crucified!* Shock, horror… Is *Skylark* blaspheming and corrupting all you readers? The answer is no! Neither is she 'devilish,' because that too is a fabrication of the word of God, my father. That, I hasten to add, is the truth… he was and is my father, but then all of you are the children of God, whether you like it or not. You may be Pagan or Wicca inspired, but God still loves you. You might be a Jew or Zoroastrian, but it is the same fatherly feelings he has for you, and so do I. My love is similar to my father's… 'his words are mine and mine are his!'

These words were channelled through Isaiah Abbotsbury, the friend and mentor of *Skylark,* one sunny day. Both knew what was spoken was important enough to hurry and write it down. Isaiah Abbotsbury is an extremely experienced soul and no pushover… similar to how I was. I had to be a strong individual, otherwise the high priest and his minions would have ridden roughshod over me… that, I couldn't allow. So, my lives built up until God knew I was ready for the one that lay ahead, where I would become known as Jesus Christ. Not my given name either… it is man-made, much like religion.

I don't mean to disillusion any of you, as the truth is more powerful than you can imagine. What *Skylark* knows, and the conclusions she has reached through her studies of scripture, are just the tip of the iceberg. No doubt, when she and Isaiah Abbotsbury get together to look at what has been transcribed, there will be questions. 'Good,' I say, otherwise how can the truth be reached. There will be one or two of us in attendance listening, and ready to channel a reply. She takes it all in her stride and so does Isaiah that is how we like it. Plain and simple, with no amateur dramatics from either of them... spot on!

To tell you a little bit of what lies ahead, in this book, is a good idea. You are going to meet apostles you have never heard of, and also hear from my friend - and apostle - Peter, who will inform you who actually founded the church in Rome. Then you will meet a man called Marcus... he was a centurion of great strength and ability. His wife, Camilla, channelled words of love, for the people of Rome to hear.

Before that, we have a handful of prophets, who will dispel a myth or two, and provide a little truth. Later on, a keeper of the Vatican library will talk about his responsibilities, many years ago, and a pope called Leo will elaborate. It doesn't matter which Leo, as they are all nearly as bad as each other.

Then, there are communicators in general, such as Florence Nightingale, Edward Benson, Tommy Cooper, and Robin Williams. These are just for starters, as Edward VI, son of Henry VIII has a little secret to impart to you... and Francis Walsingham has another. Then, we have Michael, who is similar to Francis. Michael walked the corridors of Whitehall during the cold war. Not forgetting Conan Doyle, as Sherlock Holmes has always been enjoyed by *Skylark,* no matter whom the actor... although, she does have a favourite, as I am sure many of you have.

So, I hope there is something for all, when you flick or read through the book. It has been thought about for a long period of time, and is not the first one. By the way, there are many channelled books on the open market, which are enjoyed by a vast amount of people, without them realising it was aided by spirit. The same as songs and sonatas: as Mozart had an enthusiastic guide, who inspired him and still does. He didn't know at the time, and thought he was doing well... he was! The guide was simply inspiring him and aiding him occasionally, when Mozart was struggling, which was rare.

I hope you forgive me a few personal words. The possibility

rarely occurs, and I can't but take the opportunity to do so... *you are the most amazing people on this planet, but you are not the only ones who live in the solar system. Marthera, Xavier, and Juno are three others, and they are beautiful beyond belief. You, my people, are in danger of going the opposite way, and becoming a carcass of a planet, because of your greed. If damage was caused in an attempt to explore and learn, that would be different...*

At the back of a lot of human behaviour is greed, and the rush to find and gain more. Why dig up the oceans, or at least try to? If you inhabit another planet will that be used for what it has to offer? The three mentioned above are too important to be found by you. They never will be, because of the potential of your actions, if they were. You are prepared to go to war and kill each other, in your race to gain still more. So, it truly cannot be allowed that you should ever find another planet... no matter how hard you try. You can try and perhaps think you have, but what will it be? Will it benefit you to do so, when good money can be spent on providing care for each other and helping nature? Look after this wonderful planet of yours, and she will repay you tenfold.

I am only the first that will talk to you in such a way. I will never be the last; while you contemplate the things that governments do not speak of... we know what is said, because we can listen in. We see everything that governments do not wish to be seen, and more. Can I or any other individual interfere? 'No' is the answer to that. It does mean though, that denial is of no value in spirit, when your life is shown to you on arrival. We all have to learn, and I walked this same route. If I hadn't, how do you think I would have understood the mistakes I made... or how I could have done things differently? Every action I took, I asked to be shown; I wanted to know if I could have acted to facilitate a different outcome. It is a privilege to be able to do this, because it takes strength... strength of heart and soul, and so many of you have this inside of you. Yes, a lot may scoff and deride, but some of you will know and feel the truth of what I say. That is your inner soul vibrating, and it is a good sign in your spiritual evolution.

My blessings to you all, and know this: as you walk the Earth you are not alone, as the love of heaven is with you.

JOSHUA

(30/06/17 - 17:17)

My friend and mentor was a man called Moses. I loved and respected him, and he taught me so much that I use even today. He was shrewd and physically strong, with eyes that could see into your very soul. He was like a father figure, and we often talked together in the following manner: I was saddened that he did not live to continue the very difficult task he set out to do. I finished what was given him, and was determined to do exactly that.

It was a land of plenty, with grapes, that were as the scriptures say (Numbers 13:23), but was it right of us to usurp people from the land they belonged to? Drive them from the homes they lived in? The echoes of this have played down the centuries. Yet my people needed a safe haven… a place to call home! So, I stand by what I and others did all those years ago, and I am not sorry.

Is that what you expect me to say, you the reader? You; the judge of history and what it offers? The truth is that the journey we made was far more difficult than you can imagine. So difficult, that even Moses at one stage felt that too much had been asked of him. You see, some of our people did not want to leave Egypt. They wanted what they knew, and what they didn't know was of no value to them. The squabbles and arguments would have tried the patience of a saint. No matter how much Moses endeavoured to give justice and listen to complaints, it was never enough.

Our people were greedy and stole from each other. Children would have left their parents to die at the end of a hard walk, and stole the bread from their mouths. Pagan rites abounded, with curses and spells, and men slept with their neighbour's wives and daughters. It had to stop, or else we would have become a very different people to what we are today. No surprise then that God intervened, to guide his people through the difficult days and times that lay ahead *(Exodus 20:2-17, Deuteronomy 5:6-21).*

The golden calf verses in the book named Exodus, chapter thirty-two, within the scriptures, are a story of rituals and beliefs that some of the people still clung to. It was, at the time, embedded in these people. If you think about it, Moses had a certain magic to him, and the early life of a messiah would go unnoticed in such a land as Egypt. So, the journey of a people set apart to be special to the one God had shaky foundations. Yet, it makes them human and very special.. so special, that despite everything, they are still very much in the heart of Yahweh. I too love them, and frequently visit the Dead Sea, to send healing to its waters.

Those who are more sensitive can feel this energy, which is one of love. So why is it being slowly destroyed? Used for the gains of man? The riches of the material are fleeting, yet what nature has to offer is everlasting. It is for all to enjoy. People from all over the world have stepped into the gift of the Dead Sea, and felt the salty, silky waters offer what it has to give. It has done this over the aeons of time, so it was no stranger to the people of Canaan and the surrounding area. Yet, it will slowly go the way that all nature is going on this beautiful planet... nothing will be left in its wake. I am saddened, but it is the choice of the men and women who are its guardians. I saw it in the height of its beauty, and it is a sight that I shall never forget. Over the years, as it has shrunk in diameter, its glory has never dimmed, and I hope it never does.

*****

ELIJAH

(01/07/17 - 14:09)

I was a tall man, for the time, with long flowing hair and beard. That bit might not be a surprise, but when *Skylark* saw me one day, she was surprised at how I looked. What do you expect of a prophet from long ago… a suit and Porsche? Nothing of the sort… ever! I do not enjoy the trappings of luxury, and never did in my incarnation as Elijah.

It wasn't my first life. How could it be? I would not have been able to utter prophecy if it was my first attempt. Never mind raise the widow's son (*1 Kings 17:17-24)* from a life of dust, until the day came when the dead shall rise again. That is a little bit of drama from me. I do not believe that the dead rise, because it is only the physical death of the body. If I were a dead prophet how could I speak here and now? Could *Skylark* have seen me on a clairvoyant link if my remains were lost in the Valley of Jezreel, and that was it? Simple, if you think of it like that.

Back then, people were more open to the metaphysical, as you might guess… but I still had to be careful. I often hid in caves, as the sun at noon would have burnt you in a moment. I also had to hide because I spoke the truth, at a time when it was dangerous to do so. When I showed myself to *Skylark,* I was in a cave, feeling hot, tired, and very thirsty… that was how I often felt. Sweaty, I think she thought at the time, and a bit wild and woolly-looking… like John the Baptist. I don't mind the comparison, as John is a remarkable man.

What I did back then is different to what I do now. I no longer have kings, queens and mad priests of Baal to avoid. Although, on one occasion, I did take the priests to task and won (*1Kings 18:16-39)*… with God's help, as I couldn't have done it without him. Now, that is a story to tell over dinner one evening. The priests of Baal were as crazy as crazy could be. There were odd people that roamed the mountain trails, but nothing like the priests I encountered.

I was in danger a lot of my adult life. I was too honest to be left alone, so I was hunted by paid mercenaries, until I had nowhere left to run. They began to know my hiding places, the nooks and crannies I would climb into, and the ledges I crawled across. Sometimes they lay in wait, yet God always helped me. He never left me. Even in the quiet I knew it was him (*1 Kings 19:11-13*), and that he would always be my rock; my place of refuge. So, I never wavered and walked the path laid before me. It was my choice to do this, and not God's. Just as Moses had freewill and chose to guide a lost people, so it was my choice to take God's word where it was needed. I never regretted it for an instant, when I said 'yes' to the man who asked me to help him.

God was so humble. He came to me with no flash of light or burning bush. He stood before me one hot day, with love in his heart, and I couldn't refuse. I doubted myself, but never his purpose. He trusted me, and I felt bolstered by this. So much so that I thought I could take on the world. It felt like it at times, but I always knew my limit. When I needed rest or water, sleep, food, or shade from the sun, I tried my best to follow my instinct, and it saved my life on more than one occasion.

I took his word into the depths of inequity and injustice. I experienced fear as I was human; but when I felt his spirit upon me and spoke out I knew he was guiding me, by the words I said. I wasn't an eloquent man yet he made me feel like one, and he did this all for love. Love of his people, and the promise he made to Abraham (*Genesis 12:1-3*). He wasn't going to abandon them to what the priests of Baal had in store for them. Yet, they too were human and a few were willing to walk that path... so be it. In the history of the world, Gods have come and gone, but not him. No matter the name you use, it is still love at the back of it... and that love flows ever outward, and will continue to do so.

*****

MOSES

(02/07/17 - 11:34)

I never was a prince of Egypt - of the pharaonic family that is - but I most certainly was 'well connected' in more ways than one. The pharaoh knew my name, and that was something to boast about. I was educated and spoke more than one language, yet I never fitted in. I was considered to be 'other-worldly', and that was saying something for a nation of priests and spells. Still, it helped me a lot, and meant that most of the time I was never considered a threat to the machinations of the court, and its intrigues. They knew I would never make pharaoh, so I could be left alone with my own endeavours.

My name is Moses… a name that once wielded power. It also prompted derision and scorn… and that came from my own lot… God's chosen people. The chosen people of Israel were the rudest bag of ragamuffins I ever came across, and I loved them. In every single one, I saw the light of Yahweh, and one or two loved me in return.

My brother Aaron, in the scriptures, was a social climber. Once he knew what was what, he went about making a name for himself. He tried to usurp the position which had been entrusted to me more than once. I tore a strip off him on many occasions when I caught him scheming. In his heart he was still a follower of the religion of the pharaohs… a conniver if ever there was one. I saw the fear - the insecurity - which made him behave as he did. I hoped that if I led by example, and asked nothing of him that I wouldn't do, he would walk a different path. Did he? I don't truly know, but he certainly made a name for himself in the process. My sister Miriam wasn't much different… yet in ways she was. She wasn't a fool and knew Aaron walked a different path to me. That interested her, even if it was self-interest at heart. Miriam felt the path I walked would lead to some sort of redemption. She tried herself, but it wasn't easy. She fell prey to the temptations which lay on our journey more than once.

So, my family and I were a mixed bunch, on our journey to find a home… a place to call our own, where we would be safe. Safe to follow our God and his commands… yet, are they necessary? Not the Decalogue, as that will always be of value, but the other laws which have been debated over the centuries. I mean no disrespect to Judaism or any that walk this path. Is it necessary in this day and age to separate dairy from meat? Give thanks for your bread, but do not berate yourself, or think the wrath of Yahweh will fall on your soul if you do not do it for one day. Many don't and take food for granted. That is different, as I do not like to see food wasted, and never did in my incarnation as Moses.

It doesn't mean though that you are less set apart and loved by the almighty, if the rituals of our lives are not followed to the letter. He knows and sees into your heart. If it is a busy day with time for little, he will not love you any the less for it… remember this, because we are all human, and err along the path of life. This applies to every single one of us, and we know it, because we have the feelings and associations which go with the experience. They are all an opportunity with which to grow in strength of soul. The mistakes we make on our journey give us guidance for the next one, and the one after that… so, that as our lives build up, the rituals which were once so important, give way to the spiritual journey.

Every single faith of this planet has something which is a custom, or ritual. They can and do bring you closer to God, but not always. God is not to be found in a house or steeple, but inside the heart of man. The good you do outweighs any ritual which is not a truth. This good deed or act is seen in the heavens and illumines the heart of God.

*****

GABRIEL

(08/07/17 - 17:21)

I had to think a lot about what I was going to say. *Skylark* has thought about it too, on numerous occasions. She has already worked out that angels are part of the history of the world, and not an actual fact. I thought about how not to offend or take hope away, because angels give hope and succour. Many people believe that angels exist, when I know they do not. I am considered to be a mighty one, but I am not. I never have been an angel; it is man that has made me one, and not God. What I am is an angelic-like soul. A man with love in his heart, and healing is a part of my very being. My words can heal, and the energy of my aura can do just the same. I am angelic in every sense of the word, as I am also a messenger and many other things. Do I have wings? No! Do I have a halo? No… and neither do any in the spirit plane, unless the need is there to show themselves as such.

You may perhaps think that we are deceitful, and God also? It is understandable, and I do not blame you; nor do my brothers and sisters in heaven. Angels are 'big business' on the Earth, in a lot of ways… and so are fairies. Fairies do not exist either. What does exist are hundreds and thousands of bright, evolved souls, with love and understanding, who are angelic in every way. Everything I did when thought of as an angel, I do as the man, Gabriel. Everything God asks me to do; I approach with the same love and understanding as Gabriel, the archangel.

The next two communicators are of this similar level to me. They could easily be considered archangels, but are not. Heaven is united, not made out of separate factions, with one considered to be brighter and better than another. It isn't godly, or right, to have factions in a place that is full of love and understanding. So, can you see where I am coming from, and understand the need to correct a fabrication, or belief, based on a misunderstanding which the world has gone along with?

I love each and every one of you, but this love is from Gabriel the man and evolved soul. Not the one considered to have given Mary the news of her son. It doesn't make me, or any other in heaven, less because I have spoken the truth. The truth is a powerful tool in the fight for equality and justice. It makes no sense to let the misconception about angels continue. Especially now, when the world is changing and people are yearning for truth and knowledge, about the journey their life takes them on.

Do not be alarmed by what I say, because it makes no difference whatsoever. The angelic-like souls close to the Earth are still there, and can easily be called upon if needed.

*****

ROSE

(08/07/17 - 18:08)

My credentials are quite impressive and I have a lot of experience. I am also straight-talking, which is needed under the circumstances. What are these 'credentials?' I am a highly evolved soul and I'm passionate about nature. I am also second to a man called John, and I help him look after the nature of the entire universe. So, you see I am well-connected, and have a deep understanding on the subject of your planet and its evolution. I am also friends with Charles Darwin and Patrick Moore. Both of these men are enthusiastic about their chosen subject, in their letters, when given the opportunity.

I have spoken to *Skylark* before and will do again. She knows I am straight-talking and is wondering what I am going to say. I don't pussyfoot about, so be prepared stewards of the Earth, which each of you are.

You are, step-by-step, destroying your planet, with your lack of regard, greed, and thoughtlessness. If I am honest, it disgusts me... but not you, the individual soul. As they say 'love the sinner and not the sin!' So, I love and respect you all, but not what you are doing. Do you want your children's children and their children to have a green and pleasant land? If so, then you had better get on with the job of looking after your homes more. What you drive could be far more efficient, cheaper, and kinder on nature. The crops you grow could help the birds and insects and still make you money (*note I say money, and not feed the world... but I wish they did*). Genetic modification! Oh if you only knew what I have witnessed in regard to the long-term consequences.

What you think of the weather now is just the tip of the iceberg. Each and every one of you will reincarnate. Do you want to live in places that are parched worse than areas of Africa? Do you want tornados as an everyday occurrence? Insects that cannot be controlled? The problems you have with mosquitoes will get worse in time, and will have to be dealt with, and that is just for starters. Part of the scenario could even be earthquakes... worse than previously experienced, with greater frequency. I admire your tenacity for avoiding the truth and letting business have its say, but I wouldn't want to be in your shoes when you reincarnate in the future.

...Yet I will. I will reincarnate, and do so for you. To help you look after and respect this beautiful planet that *you* control. It will not be yet, as things have to get worse first, before I will be listened to. You know the format from your films in the cinema. It always has to get worse before anybody does anything. So, I will come when things deteriorate... and I will. Do not think that I won't, because I shall. My gender will be of no significance to me, but as it's the Earth I am talking about, I had better be male... the best way to be heard, I have witnessed. Do not look for me, as that will do no good... I won't know I am *'me'*... avoids the ego you see.

My voice will be heard, as I will study at university and will work hard, so I know my subject. Those of you who are listening will hear it, and feel the truth of what I say. I will also be able to back it up with facts and figures, and my years of research in this role will help a lot. I am a determined soul and good for you that I am, because I can help you more. This determination will be part of my Earth character, as I have asked for it to be. I have choice in some things in this life, and the rest is what's needed at the time. You will meet me again and again in the books, as I will not give up. I hope I never become the voice you do not wish to hear. If I do, then perhaps I am making my mark, and getting you to think about the Earth and what you are doing. Until we meet again, I wish you the joy in the life you walk, and may God be with you,

Rose

CHRISTOPHER

THE JOURNEY'S END
(10/07/17 - 12:35)

I am a tall man and quite grey. My height and hair is of no consequence, because the reality is that I only show myself in human form on levels one and two, in spirit. Otherwise I have no Earthly body whatsoever, because it is not needed on the higher levels… especially not on level seven, which is where I am from. It is the energy we bring with us that is important, and not how tall we are or our hair colour. In levels one and two you will find the least experienced souls. I need to use the above description when I am there, so they can see who I am.

There are lots of people on these levels who are keen to learn and one of them is a man called Christopher Hitchins. He is a delightful soul, enthusiastic to learn more and be of service, so he can help other people. You will also find the Halls of Rest on level one, which is where I come into things… partly anyway.

This piece is called 'the journey's end' for a reason. It is my responsibility, when you pass to spirit - at the correct stage of your life - that you are surrounded by love, with no hiccups, or getting lost on your way. It is a journey that all have to make, so it's up to me and my merry team of helpers to make sure that you are not alone. I have a lot of experienced angelic-like souls to help me. I also have a lot of willing and enthusiastic helpers, who are learning at the same time. Christopher Hitchins is one of these, along with the father of your current queen, in the United Kingdom. These men are not the only ones, as many of your friends and relatives want to give what they were given, and that is a helping hand on the path of life. Nobody needs to be qualified, and I never say 'no', as the experienced members of my team will guide and train the new ones, before they work with them.

The process, from my end, is straightforward, as the experienced soul will be the one in the forefront, who will take your hand and guide you on your way; with absent healing being sent by the helper in the background. Sometimes a person might look to be by themselves at the time of their passing, but the reality is that we are always ready, and a loved one is usually close by, waiting in the wings. Quite often a much loved pet, in spirit, will rush forward and say hello expecting a pat or a stroke in the process. It helps so much when the animal is recognised, because joy fills the heart, and it is only moments then until the Halls of Rest is reached.

The Halls of Rest are found on level one. It is the place you all go to - like a reception area - where loved ones are waiting, and you can acclimatise to your new life from there. As well as loved ones, there are many skilled clinicians and counsellors. Not everyone recognises the hand of friendship or the emotion of love and can maybe have emotional problems, as a result. So, we have advanced souls with a deep understanding of the human psyche, ready to help if called upon.

There is one area of the spirit plane that we cannot allow access to willy-nilly, and that is the lower levels. It is only the brightest and most experienced soul - helping the unenlightened and nefarious individuals - who have gravitated to where it is most appropriate for them to be. I am sure you understand why access is limited. Quite often these individuals lie and say that it is not their fault. But, you see, they cannot lie to us, as we see things differently and will have tracked them during their Earth life, and recorded what they have done. Lies and denial do not work here, unlike the Earth. Raphael is in control of these levels and he will explain more in his letter later on.

I would now, if you don't mind, like to explain about children that pass to spirit. Your sons and daughters are loved and cherished and given everything that any child on the Earth is given. Your family and friends help them to grow up and love them every bit as much as you do. This means they are able to play, meet other children and go to school. We have every facility possible to help a child achieve and fulfil their personal dreams.

Sometimes a little one will come to heaven unloved, but not so here. Never is a child left abandoned or in the hands of strangers. There is always love from us and especially from Mary, the mother of Jesus. She is often with the children, to talk to them, tell stories and help find a new family to be with. Mary is vigilant, but it is not a difficult process, because we see so many willing people, by the light of their soul. We see their goodness and know they will give the love and support needed. That is of paramount importance.

The journey you make to heaven is a glorious one, of light and love, with friends and family ready to welcome you. As you make your journey, you will be on the wings of love with each step you make.

Christopher

ADU

LOVE
(13/07/17 - 15:48)

Love comes in all sorts of different forms, shapes, and sizes. It came to me one day and asked me if I wanted to be bought… this was by a man called Joseph of Arimathea. A tall Jew with a son called Abraham. I looked at him and my heart sang. I never wanted to be a slave and felt that if he became my master, I never would be… I was correct. Joseph said that I was free to do as I pleased, but that his son needed a man to protect him and be his friend and mentor. I asked him 'why me? I could leave and never look back and you would have lost your money.' He said 'friend, I know you are that man,' and I was. I guarded Abraham with my life until I met Jesus and stood by his side.

Joseph and his wife Sarah were rich beyond your wildest dreams. That is why Abraham needed a man to walk with, and guard him from thieves and ruffians. He was not a well boy, and illness came to him that nearly took his life. Jesus helped, but that is for another day my friends, because now I need to tell you something of my story.

I have been removed from the scriptures, along with the other three who follow me in the book. We each have a story to tell, and I will give you an idea of mine. Just an idea, as I do not have the time to tell my life's history to you… not now anyway.

As a child growing up, in what is now called Ethiopia, I was unlike other boys. I did not want to hunt or kill and I would not take the life of another man. I was thought a coward, and 'like a girl' by my brothers. My grandfather knew different and said to my father 'give him to me and I will show you what kind of man he will become.' That is what my father did and I outshone even the son he was the proudest of. I have never killed another man and only ever hunted for food; never for pleasure. Yet, I made my brothers look like they were the cowardly ones.

My grandfather knew I was different. I would say to him 'why do I see the colour of the sun around you as a bright glow, yet I can look at

31

it without flinching?' My grandfather saw what I saw. He could see men walk that he knew were killed by another's hand. He saw the colour of the sun around men and women, and blues like the sea. He dreamed of dead men talking... I did this and more! Grandfather would say to me that dead men do not talk, it is only the living that do. Yet he listened to what the men who were 'no more' had to say, and knew they lived. He would say to me 'you are special my son and men will try to kill you for this, so I must teach you what to do.'

What he showed me I taught to Abraham, and it helped save his life more than once. Yet, on one occasion, there was a slave trader with a man that could track like no other, and I was caught, bound and taken to be sold. Joseph of Arimathea bought me and I saw the blue of the sea in his eyes, and around his head the gold of a man of mercy. I knew he would never torture or beat me, so I said yes to his proposition.

That is only a little of my history my friends, but I will say more on other occasions about my life with Abraham, and how we met again in Rome. I will also tell you a little about Jesus and my time with him. Joseph knew when Jesus came to speak with me that I would go. I did, but I never forgot the family who gave me a home and treated me like a brother.

*****

DEBORAH

I am the daughter of a rich merchant of Tyre, considered to be spoilt and intelligent. I was a Pagan, of course, until I met the prophet and married his friend Thomas. Thomas was thought to doubt, but he never did with me. We looked at each other, and knew that despite our different backgrounds we would be together forever.

I am an apostle! I want this heard, so it cannot be forgotten, again! Like Adu, I was removed from the writings of old, destined to be shelved… or so they thought! I have a voice, and I intend to use it here on this page, and will shock you, if I haven't done so already. Those of you who doubt what you are reading, I say that peace will flow into your hearts and then see how you feel. You may still be unsure, if that is your nature and doctrine. I do not blame you, but you will have more to contend with on the pages that follow, and I laugh at the thought of it. Not cruelly, as that is not in the nature of any apostle; but with joy. Yes, joy, because I can see that it will make you think, perhaps even want to know more, and that can only be good. Good for your evolution and the future of the Earth.

God likes a challenge and so did Thomas. He never shirked from what God or Jesus asked of him. I went with him, after we married, to places I had never heard of and thought didn't exist… yet, they did indeed. I mastered every language I needed to, with God's help, and so did Thomas. The Chinese people called him 'laughing bear' because of his frame, his booming voice and laugh. They loved him and so did I! Together with our family, we took the word to where we were guided. Up mountains and along the rivers of life. To dirty cities with their cruelties and licentiousness. It made no difference… if we were needed that is where we went. We made friends along the way, and became a happy group of travellers, along the path of life.

It wasn't easy to begin with. Thomas had a large family, and they were not happy about his time with Jesus… never mind marrying a pagan idolatrous! His mother was different… she wanted Thomas to be happy and could see that, with me, he was. He was her favourite; her pride and joy. Because her love was true she let him go, never to see him again… or so she thought.

Then we had the temple spies to contend with, as Thomas was a well-known teacher. The long reach of Caiaphas was nearly as bad as Rome, but God looked after us, and we survived all attempts at ending our lives prematurely.

My family were different. My mother was dead and my father loved me, and could never say 'no' to anything I wanted. He nearly did this time, but it was out of love for me that he changed his mind. He thought I would be unhappy in a land with people who had strange ways. Inside his heart, he knew he would miss me and didn't want me to leave. I told him that no matter where I was, he would always be inside my heart. He knew I spoke the truth, and he gave us a generous dowry, with his blessings. I did miss my father, I thought of him often, and knew that time and distance would never separate us, at the end of our journey.

So, a female became an apostle, but was taken out of a book destined to be read by millions. Yet, I am not the only one to be treated so… not the only woman either! You will meet a few upon the pages of this book and more. It will show you that the early foundations of Christianity were built upon the hard work of men and woman… that **women were seen as equals in the eyes of God…** if you think about it, how can it be any other? Is God unequal in his love? You know the answer to this; I do not have to spell it out! So, why do women have to work so hard to be accepted in the Christian Church of this Earth? A woman can minster in any faith, on any road to salvation. We all have something to offer, and I found this out on my journey with Thomas. It taught me so much that I use even now, to try to help you all.

I cannot make your minds up for you, but listen, and you will hear what you do not expect; and that is words of love, from the women of the early church.

Amen

A WALK WITH SEBASTIAN

(05/08/17 - 15:33)

I am a tall, gangly looking man, who liked to walk a lot. I had no choice as my feet were the only way I could go from 'a' to 'b'. It didn't matter, because walking always gave me time to think. I could have a problem, and by the end of the day, I had worked it out by walking it off… so, walking to Rome, at the call of God, didn't faze me that much.

What did bother me were my wife and daughter. I could easily fend for myself, but with the things we may encounter, I didn't want to endanger them. I wanted us to have a place to sleep for the night and a warm meal, but I couldn't promise it. They both said they would come with me, no matter what. I was pleased at that, because I loved them and didn't want to leave them behind. Rome was different though. Did I really want to take my family from Pamphylia to the centre of the known world… a place famous for injustice and cruelty? No, I did not, but I felt that God had a role for all of us, so did they.

The call of God can be a strange thing. I often wondered if I had imagined it, but I didn't imagine the feeling of love when he was near. As we walked, so I thought he walked with us… more than once we avoided danger, and I don't know how. Perhaps I do as I reflect; we had many coincidences on our journey.

We had help from people we never expected, and quite often the offer of somewhere to sleep. I did a little work, so I could repay one or two for their generosity, and I always tried to be of service, if I could. It felt natural to be generous and kind, rather than avaricious and rude. It made the day better, but I was wise enough not to be taken for granted, and was rarely cheated. The ins and outs of our journey I will not bother with. It was long and tiring, as you might expect; but as for the rest, it is all in the Halls of Learning, in the books there, and freely available for any to read. It is of course - or some of it - documented here on the Earth. Little snippets of it, on fragments of parchment, held under the strictest of conditions, which can be easily denied, if needed… a little cloak-and-dagger sounding to some of you maybe? Well, give it time, the truth will always out, and you can choose to read it in spirit, whenever you want to. You can also meet all of us, who were removed from the life and times of the early church, and there are more of us than you think.

There is also a tremendous amount none of you know about Jesus and his friends, Marcus and Flavius... never mind Joseph of Arimathea and Adu... I could write a book on it... never mind *Skylark,* or the transcribers who will follow her. There is a lot to get down and it will take more than *Skylark* to do it.

The history of the church has been given a lot of thought, by men who were involved, and we did not exclude the women and their stories. The women will have a voice, and some of you may not like it. 'Good,' is my opinion on that! Camilla, the wife of Marcus, was an amazing woman who channelled God's love the same as any man did, and her documented healings have gone unnoticed. Not for long, as *Skylark* has already taken one down in the first draft of this book, and she will document more. Ask her about Camilla and Demetrius; it might make you think... except *Skylark* prefers to be more discreet than that, so you might never get to meet her, if she has her way. We will do our best with this, but she knows we cannot guarantee anonymity for her lifetime, because of freewill... still, we can try!

At our journeys end lay Rome, and I wasn't sure what came after that. We entered the city on a hot, busy day, with people bustling about and generally being rude to all and sunder. More than once, I felt a hand leave my garments without pickings, as I had nothing to give, never mind steal. I needn't have worried though, as God had thought it all through. He had planned our entry into a world we didn't know existed, and they were waiting for us... Marcus and Camilla, Flavius and his wife Junia, had been told by God that we were making our way to them, and would be in need of help when we arrived. We were not disappointed, and our journey had not been for nothing. I cannot say more than this at the moment, as the apostle Peter has to explain one or two things, and he will not be long in doing so.

What I can finish on is, that I hope our walk together has intrigued you; maybe challenged you a little. Remember this though, that it is my words and not *Skylark's* that you read on the page. I choose what I feel is appropriate to say at this moment, because of the level of understanding there is about the apostles and their stories. If I were to blab away, then it could deter a lot of you from wanting to know more. So, step-by-step, you will hear a lot that you never expected to.

I bless you all, and hope that your journeys are as fulfilling as mine and my families.

Sebastian

FLAVIUS - A SPANIARD IN ROME

(09/08/17 - 12:08)

I was part of the Roman army once - nothing special - never an officer. I wanted a family, so I joined the legions when I could. My brother, Antony, became a gangster and brothel owner, in Rome's underbelly. It was in the army that I met a man who would change my life forever. His name is Marcus; he became a father to me, and I loved him as one.

I am now an apostle and my brother is a reformed man - keen to help and not hinder - and be a light to others. It wasn't easy for him to escape the only family he had ever known, in the gangs, and he liked the power he had. His journey is for him to tell, but we met as men after many years, and fought as such. I asked him to meet my family afterwards and the rest, as they say, is history.

Antony thought he had found what he wanted in life, when we went our separate ways; but I knew for sure that I had, because of where it led me. I am not talking about battles and war… few of us liked that. I found acceptance and the next thing to family, and I made a friend in Marcus, that I knew would be forever. I also met others I liked in the army, and we looked out for each other on many occasions.

I am scarred, as you might expect, from war and the punishment inflicted by my fellow soldiers. Nothing unusual… it is what it is! A severe beating was sometimes given if you didn't toe the line; preferable as it wouldn't involve senior officers, and quite often sorted things out. I do not condone such behaviour… neither did Marcus, but I know of one or two occasions when he did condone it, in order to protect the lives of innocent people. He hoped, on these occasions, that it would warn the soldiers, that if they continued to behave in such a way, he would not be able to save them. He was the fairest of men, but not a fool. If the men had a problem they knew they could go to him. As for me, I trusted him with my life and he trusted me likewise.

I do not want to say too much, as I shall give all away. Perhaps one or two of you are reading between the lines, and seeing what I and others are saying. Maybe your guides are helping you? But be patient, and you will read more soon. I have a lot to tell you, but the truth needs to come first - before my story - as without it, nothing will make sense. I can say one thing though, and that is, I helped Jesus avoid the road to Golgotha. A few of us did, Marcus included, and it didn't go down well with some of the officials in the Sanhedrin. They couldn't prove it, but tried their best. Luckily Pilate had met Jesus, and he didn't like Caiaphas, and a few others he had come into contact with. He was in fine political form for an ill and dying man, when Caiaphas came in, full bluster, to complain. I heard rumours that the shouting between them could be clearly heard, with threats coming from either side.

It is difficult for *Skylark* to write this piece, as she has just said to me that she knows too much and is anticipating what I am going to say. Yes, she knows something, but not everything, as there is a whole lot more to explain. I hope when she sees the fuller picture, it will illumine her heart and soul. I pray that it will do the same for all of you.

Flavius

GOD

NOT IN MY NAME
(13/08/17 - 08:03)

There is the saying *'love the sinner and not the sin.'* I am not a God of sin and obedience, so I do not love the sinner, because I do not agree with this statement. I love each and every one of you, but I have to make clear to you all that murder is an act that requires karmic consequences. *'Not in my name'* also means that no war should ever be started with the idea that **I AM*** is on the side of the winner. I never will be, as I do not condone the taking of life whatsoever.

This also applies to any courtroom around the world - it makes no difference its name - but if the ultimate price is to be paid, then it is the law of the land that requires it, and not me. I love you all, but you have to understand that you cannot do deeds in my name, that I am not part of. What you do, you do for yourselves, and not in defence of - or for - me. The law of the land is just that, quite simply. All of the Messiahs that walked this Earth followed it, as they had no choice but to do that. Yet, they could not stand idly by and watch injustice and cruelty take place… neither can I.

When a drug dealer pushes a drug onto another fellow human; when they use 'mules' or groom a person into nefarious deeds, they do so from now on with the understanding that it will impact their karma, ten times over. I say 'ten times' because the understanding has to be a deep one, in order to make clear all of its consequences.

Karma is fair and just, and nothing to do with me, as it is up to the individual what they do. Sometimes we may feel emotional because of what life has offered us, and perhaps could be thinking negatively. Karma will take into account every aspect of the Earth life before it responds. I say 'responds' because that is exactly what it is… a response! So, if you are a greedy drug dealer, 'in it for the money,' woe betide you in your next life. Turn your face to the light of eternal life, and you will see a different reaction to your needs and requirements. If you are a terrorist, thinking you are acting in my name then remember this…

YOU ARE NOT! You will see and feel what you have done in the lower levels of the spirit plane, just the same as all the others have.

I cannot stress how much I love you, my people, but this planet is the worst I have witnessed for injustice and cruelty, greed and corruption. I have to speak like this because I want to help you, and help you to be kind to other people. Kindness is not about being weak, but being generous and strong, with wisdom guiding you in your actions; so you are not taken for granted or misused. It takes strength also to seek help; it is not being feeble of heart and mind. I bless all of you and know the good that is done, because I see it and say thank you to the people of every nation who are kind and generous.

I say to the traffickers of human lives, *'think what you are doing… you cannot take your riches to heaven, and your power is only fleeting… it is nothing compared to the love of the spirit plane. Every life is sacred and of great importance, so when you push a refugee overboard and do not care; do you think I will be like that when you face me many years ahead? Is your life worth more than theirs? When you traffic in slaves do you think I will make you a slave to your karma? I do not need to and never would, as you will do it for yourselves, with your greed and injustice!'*

You may think that *Skylark* is making all of this up, well, that is for you to decide, and your freewill upon this Earth. But you *will* know, because I shall make sure that you do so… you have the opportunity to think differently and behave accordingly. Your guides will help you to see the consequences, and the rest is up to you.

You see, every single person on this Earth has a guide, who is there to inspire, send healing and help you to fulfil the karma of your current life. So, what do you think their thoughts are when they look at you, if you walk the path of inequity? Do they still love you? Respect you? I leave you to ponder on that, but if you have understood what I have said so far, you will know the answer.

Lastly, I say to the men and women who throw acid into another's face… *'do you think I will throw your lives into your faces, when you see me many years from now?'*

Remember my people... *that karma is not about injustice or cruelty, and neither am I.*

*   *'I AM WHO I AM'*

Then Moses said to God, 'if I come to the people of Israel and say to them, "The God of your fathers has sent me to you," and they ask me, "What is his name?" What shall I say to them?' God said to Moses, 'I AM WHO I AM!' And he said, 'Say this to the people of Israel, "I AM has sent me to you."' God also said to Moses, 'say this to the people of Israel, "The Lord, the God of your fathers, the God of Abraham, the God of Isaac, and the God of Jacob, has sent me to you." This is my name forever, and thus I am to be remembered throughout all generations.' (Exodus 3:13-15).

*****

PETER

THE WHOLE TRUTH... AND NOTHING BUT THE TRUTH
(13/08/17 - 11.42)

The truth is sometimes a difficult story to tell. Gabriel has spoken it and so have all the communicators, but do you want to hear what I have to say? Do you want to feel challenged? Well if you do, then read on... if not, think and reflect, and you may change your mind. If you are not bothered, then neither am I... except that I am!

I want to tell you the truth of what has been hidden for so long. Isaiah Abbotsbury and his wife Tilly know a little, and *Skylark* knows more. None of them though know the full amount of what I am about to say, or what I will talk about in the future. I intend to make the letter short and bit-by-bit speak to you more on the subject; along with details about my life in general. The others involved will do the same.

So, I had better get straight to the point... ***I did not commence the church in Rome!*** Did I help? Yes, of course I did, and so did Paul... but the people who worked so hard for the men and women, oppressed and downtrodden, were led by a man called Marcus and his wife Camilla.

Marcus and Camilla were the brightest of the bright... strong and courageous people... not afraid to walk where angels fear to tread... but they were not the only ones.

Flavius was a tower of strength to Marcus, and his wife Junia was the blessing of Rome. *What a wonderful way to be remembered... as a blessing!* Then there is Demetrius, and Sebastian and his family. Pontius Pilate, before he died, reached out to another level of Roman officials. They openly scoffed, but then came in darkness, to visit a man, not afraid, and happy to meet his God... and they are just for starters.

Was I imprisoned in Rome? 'No,' and neither was Paul. We were both free men, and when we moved to pastures new, we lived long and happy lives with our families. God manifested for a human life. He supported Marcus and Camilla, and all of the apostles and their co-workers in Rome. To be expected, as he has walked the streets of Aleppo, and been shot at by snipers, who did not know the person they were aiming at could not be killed. If they did, do you think it would have made any difference? He goes where many fear to walk. He has been into the depths of the cruellest organisations of this world, and the most secret. Nothing deters him. So, it was natural that he would do what he could to help in Rome... and he did!

I will leave what I have said so far to percolate, and for you to peruse over. There is more my friends... always more. If you want to know, then stay with us for the journey of a lifetime.

Peter

MARCUS

NEW BEGINNINGS
(13/08/17 - 12:47)

What a shocker, to know that the church in Rome was based on a misunderstanding; the fault of which lies with the individuals concerned. They have now faced the truth and accepted it, moved on and learnt the value of the spoken and written word. As I channel, I have pondered long and hard about what I will say. This opportunity cannot be wasted. I have asked Camilla what she thinks, and she has been forthright as usual. What she says though, she always has love and goodness at the back of her words. So, she has asked me to send absent healing to *Skylark,* who is facing her pathway and karma with determination.

As I send this so-called 'absent healing' (*because the healing isn't absent)* to *Skylark,* so you will also receive it as you read, because its essence will be in each part of the word of God; no matter what. For me, the source of the energy of the world is God and his love for you. It surrounds us all in spirit and lifts us to new levels. Even the grumpy and nefarious souls on the lower levels get surrounded by it, from time to time… and they don't always like it! 'Tough' I say. If it will help to move them forward and open to the light, and not the darkness, then so be it. It is part of their karma, and ours, that we have to try to help, in every way possible.

That is how I felt about Rome, its people and its emperors. I wanted to help all I could and so did Camilla; my rock and my inspiration. She was a leader of the church in Rome, and the movement, yet denied any involvement in it. Back then, we did not think of it as a 'church.' It is what it has become, but wasn't intended to be. Originally we were to inspire, and show by deed and thought a new and better way of life, than degradation and ill will to neighbours and the world in general.

Over the years this has turned from a way of life into a money-making venture, with corruption manifest in its heart, as the politics grew. Yet, I cannot and will not believe this entirely. I know and see people go out of their way to help, to minister and go the extra mile. In spite of the fact I have witnessed corruption in popes and cardinals, bishops and vicars, and the people who help them. Does power corrupt? Does it mean that every pope or Archbishop of Canterbury has greed in their heart? The answer to this is a resounding **'*no*,'** and I say again, **'*no*.'**

Edward Benson is one example, and Justin Welby is another… both of these men are leaders, with love in their hearts, ready to help wherever they can. One might be in spirit, but Edward will minister and give of his soul, and shines with the joy of it. I also see a lot of people in the churches of the world shine in this same manner, and I rejoice when I do. It encourages me to strive harder and help you as much as I can. We all feel like this, and that is partly why this book of letters is being written now. It gives time for it to be read, mulled over and digested, along with the other writings, ready for the incarnation of Rose. She is coming to help you.

Rose is a forthright lady, like Camilla, who will be supported by us in spirit. We do this for the love of you. Just as Jesus reincarnated out of love, so will Rose. Each bright and evolved soul in the spirit plane sends absent healing to the Earth. Not all of you feel it because you are not sensitive enough, but ask *Skylark* about the Dead Sea and she will tell you what it feels like.

When I was in Rome, I never went anywhere without sending absent healing to the people or situation I was going to. Sometimes I felt frustrated, because I thought *why isn't this working?* Then I began to realise the subtleties of the energy and its potential, and slowly I saw things change. I saw the blind see and the deaf hear. I watched men and women downtrodden, lift their heads up with pride. I saw God minister to children with such gentleness, as he bathed sores and tended wounds. He did whatever I asked of him, and more. Then I witnessed miracles, which have been documented, but hidden away. How could a woman such as Camilla channel healing and heal, as Jesus did? This was too much for some early church writers and theologians to understand.

Now though, you will read as much as *Skylark* can write in her lifetime; coupled with letters from the likes of Cary Grant, Freddie Mercury and Margery Allingham in this book; you will also read letters

46

from Julius Caesar, Cicero and Saint Francis of Assisi in future books. A group of different people, yet they all have something to say, which we hope will be of interest. Their backgrounds are varied but with one common goal, and that is the good of the Earth and her peoples. Freddie is a wonderful soul, who will talk to anybody and brings joy with him, and Julius no longer uses any titles and has reincarnated since many times.

As for me, an ex-centurion of the legions and an apostle, I wish you the joy of your pathway, and may God be with you until we talk again.

*****

EDWARD BENSON

IT TOOK TIME
(02/09/17 - 11:37)

My journey has been fascinating to me. I loved my life as Archbishop of Canterbury, but as I reflect, I wish I hadn't occasionally preached about sin and obedience. I supported each archbishop who came after me, by sending absent healing, and I support the current Archbishop of Canterbury in this same manner. I have looked back on my lives, and like Yeshua, wondered how I could have done things differently; including my preaching.

Sin and obedience never have formed God's love. I have done neither in heaven, and God has not asked me to be loyal and faithful to him. I choose to out of genuine love, which requires no genuflection to a cross, or other such definition or interpretation, demonstrated by man. The power of the cross has been debated, written about and felt, but the cross was not Jesus' fate, as he was helped to escape it. He would though have looked his karma in the face, with courage and determination, and accepted whatever it gave to him. This means of death was intended by Caiaphas, his siblings and family, but not followed through out of love (which Caiaphas did not have in his heart for anybody… not even God).

When I first arrived in the Halls of Rest it was a puzzle indeed. I did not know where I was, or how I felt about what I witnessed. It took me sometime to adjust to my surroundings. When I did, then the questions poured out of me, as love flowed into my heart and soul. I wanted to know why Jesus wasn't crucified, when it was the foundation of my faith. Note, I say faith, as I don't think I loved God then, as I do now. I also wanted to know why Jesus had a disabled brother, when the scriptures said nothing about it. I asked and asked all manner of things, until I felt comfortable with my understanding; comfortable enough to read the originals in their lingua franca.* I wanted to miss nothing, so I learnt what I needed, in order to help me move forward further.

I have seen everything written about the life of Jesus and the early movement. The men and women astounded and amazed me, and I love them for it. I love the fact that I was challenged, as without it I might never have known the truth. I might also not have the relationship I have with God and Simon (the brother of Jesus, I mentioned earlier). I would not be speaking to you now either, and that is a privilege I feel honoured to accept.

In heaven there still are popes and cardinals, vicars and archbishops; unable to step forward and ask what they think is unforgivable. I did not shy away from it, but it was difficult... very much so. I felt I was being defiant and a heretic, and that the proverbial *wrath of God* would fall upon me. Yet it never did - quite the opposite - and so much so that I felt emboldened to ask more and more, until now, where I help the men and women who struggle with their journey of salvation.

The fact that I was an Archbishop of Canterbury helps, but I only use the title if I have to. Just the same as Diana, Princess of Wales... she will only use hers for the benefit of the individual, and for no other reason... and I follow her with this. Titles are of no privilege here, which has surprised the odd duke or two, but it is for the best. The light of the inner soul says what it needs to, and nothing else.

So where am I now? Happy. So happy that I can't begin to describe the joy I feel at my new enlightened state, brought on by facing the challenges of a new understanding, which is one of truth. I will add one more thing before I begin my final paragraph, and that is... *do not believe just because I and others in this book have spoken of our experiences. I do not want what I have said to be taken as gospel, as it is my journey and not the word of God (which will come later on again). It is not his words, but mine, and my experiences that I transmit, and no others. You must do as you will with them. It is the gift within your soul to see as you wish to.*

I do not spend my time involved with the Christian faith all day, every day. I do other things, as I have learnt to channel the healing energy. At the moment my focus is on the Middle East. I have many friends from Iraq and Syria in heaven, and I go with them to channel healing, and give help where needed, as best I can. It is difficult as you may imagine, but none of us are deterred by what we see and experience in these countries. God is our inspiration in so many ways, and he can be no other. If he is not prepared to enter into a prison, anywhere in the world, to bring hope and healing, then why should it be demanded of us? It never is and never would be.

What I do, I do for the love of my Iraqi and Syrian friends, and the plight of their families, still on the Earth. I go with purpose and hope, and bring the love channelled by God with me. I am not alone, as people from many nations are focused on the Middle East, along with other areas of this beautiful world. A world of such potential, yet whose people dig deep into the chaos of destruction. It will not always be so. Those of you who help, minister and give of your heart and soul are seen by us, in heaven, and we bless you, each and every one. For what you do may go unnoticed, but not by God or the enlightened souls with him.

May the blessings of God be with you all. May his face look upon you and bring joy to the road ahead.

Edward

*   *A language that is adopted as a common language, between speakers whose native languages are different. Historically, a mixture of Italian, French, Greek, Arabic and Spanish: formerly used in the Mediterranean.*

MUMTAZ

(10/10/17 - 15:19)

I am a happy soul… now, that is. I wasn't so, as a woman in Iraq, a few years ago. I loved my sons but not my husband or parents, and I didn't particularly like my siblings. So, what has happened to make me into who I am now? 'A lot' is the answer, but I needed help from a few people in spirit.

Here is a little of my story, and I feel it is important because I am accepted for who I am, and loved by people of different nations and identities. I died during the invasion of Iraq. I wasn't the only one, as my parents and children died too, along with my husband. We were not a happy family, but who was back then? The bombings were terrifying, and so were Saddam's spies and blackmailers. That is all in the past now, for me and my sons, as we have new lives, full of opportunities, that we would never have had living in Iraq. I have divorced my husband and we only speak if we have to… and that is rare.

I was given, by my parents, to a man who didn't love me, and I have not yet forgiven him for the treatment I received at his hands. Neither have I forgiven my parents, as they knew what they were letting me in for. I have let go of a lot though, with the aid of a counsellor in the Halls of Rest, who stood by my side when I said that I wanted nothing more to do with him. She also supported me when I spoke to my family, about the abuse I received at their hands. I thank her from the bottom of my heart for her kindness and generosity. Let me tell you that I am not bitter, it is what it is, and although forgiveness is a journey in itself, I have made a life and have a new family and career in spirit.

When I was in the Halls of Rest, acclimatising to my new situation, I felt myself being sent absent healing from a development group on the Earth plane. It changed my life and woke me to my new surroundings. I was not the only Iraqi, as we were their focus, and they do not know how the energy they channelled has helped us. It is not for every development group to perform this kind of work, as it takes a skilled soul to guide the group, and they had one. The name of this individual is Isaiah Abbotsbury. It will be a surprise to him to read this, but it changed a lot of Iraqi lives, in spirit, for the better.

So, I divorced my husband and separated myself from my family, and then wondered what to do with my life; as what I did would impact on my sons. I need never have worried, as a family I had become friends with asked me to join them, and be part of their family. I said 'yes' with no backward glance. I looked to the future with them and took their name, and love blossomed in my heart. We are a mixed group of people from England, Northern Ireland, Somalia, Australia, and Iraq, and I love them all for what they gave to me and my sons. Both of my boys are sons to be proud of; loved and supported by their new family - who accepted me - they love them as though they are their own.

Heaven is like that though, and so is God. If I were to say that God spoke to me personally, would you believe it? Do you believe what I said about Isaiah Abbotsbury and his development group? Or about the family who asked me to be with them? What I say is from my heart and soul, and although it may sound like a story, I speak so the world knows that Iraq is loved and not forgotten about.

My life now has changed beyond belief, as I am a qualified veterinary surgeon, specialising in cats. My sons are both training to be doctors, hoping to specialise in psychiatry and rheumatology. We can do this in spirit, and the experience we gain will help future lives we choose to live, thereby helping the world. Do you know what this means to me, to know that I and my family can help the future of the world? It means a lot. I am not the only one, as from my country, there are people training to be physiotherapists, beekeepers, lawyers, farmers, and a lot are learning about the oceans and sea so they can help Cuttlefish and Waterlily (two developed souls responsible for the waters of the world). We do this for you and this beautiful world. If only you could see what I do from spirit, then you would not throw rubbish away willy-nilly, or consume in the way that many of you do.

When I next reincarnate, I shall be a veterinary surgeon, and use what I have learnt to good effect; but I shall not stop at that. I also hope to become a beekeeper and nature enthusiast with, I hope, a partner by my side, who shares my love of nature and wildlife. I want to help Rose as much as I can, and although I am not sure if I will reincarnate when she does, I still hope I have something to offer. From where I have come from that is a gift I cannot refuse, and I look forward to being able to give of my heart and soul, to the people I meet.

*****

(PRINCESS) DIANA

A NEW PERSPECTIVE
(10/10/17 - 16:33)

Do not expect the unexpected from me, as that will be for ears other than you the reader. I mean no offence when I say this, and I know that *Skylark* is in agreement with me; as neither of us wants this piece to be one of notoriety. I will say one thing that I expect you all know, and that is, *'I love my sons so very, very much, and I am extremely proud of them.'* I would also like to say hello to a friend who will one day see me, and add to this by saying, *'I may be enshrined in a heart, but I am alive with every fibre of my being'*... that is for my friend to work out, but they will know without too much thought.

So, what is the point of my letter, if I have nothing to reveal, which will add to the gossip columns of the newspapers? I am done with all that, as the pretentiousness of the celebrity status has no value here, and neither does money or rank. What does matter is what I do and how I live my life, where the values are different to what I was used to. I had my own standards and tried to live by them, but it wasn't always easy, as I was human in many ways.

All of us have opportunities that we can accept or decline; such is the nature of freewill. One of these was to let bygones be bygones, and start afresh in a lot of ways. I had my misunderstandings with family and friends, but that is all in the past. I like this very much, as I am accepted for me. I am on good terms with a lot of people, and Mary of Teck is one of them. You may think of her as Queen Mary, and will hear from her later in the book. She is one of the loveliest people, who has a high regard for the United Kingdom; so much so that it is on her list of countries which she sends absent healing to.

Mary - or May, as she likes to be called - is a busy worker for the good of many nations, along with her husband George. It could be a surprise to hear of members of the royal family in this way. Not to us in heaven, as we pull together for the good of the Earth, no matter where that may be.

But, what do I do? As I have not been wasting my time, idling my days away. I help in the Halls of Rest, as much as possible. I go in the simplest of terms, to try to help a person, if they are struggling to understand where they are. Quite often, all I need to do is send absent healing, especially if a relative of theirs is nearby, who they know has passed on. Then the understanding comes, and off they go with their guide and family member, to learn in greater detail about their new life and karma. I enjoy this work, as I know it is of benefit... as it benefitted me a lot.

I have also learnt more about meditation. It is a discipline that requires time and effort, and the understanding of the correct way to go about it. I went to the Halls of Learning and found a development group, and guide, to teach me. It took some practice, but now I feel the benefit of meditation, when time allows. I say 'when time allows,' as I also like to be near to my family, and send healing to the Earth, to help the troubled areas.

It is possible to achieve a lot, because the energy in heaven is lighter and brighter than the Earth, so we can appear to be in more than one place at the same time. Movement is simple too, as it barely requires any thought. The only thing is, that nearer to the Earth the denser the energy, but it still means that it is possible to move faster than the human eye can see. So it's easy for me to be with family, and be able to do other things.

Do not be surprised when I say I am with my family, as wouldn't you want to be with yours, if you could? A lot of your relatives are with you, but cannot interfere, as it is your life and daily tasks, and not theirs. It is important to remember this, as it is not the role of any in heaven to rule your life, no matter how much they love you. Sometimes people misunderstand this in their enthusiasm, but it is still not acceptable to behave in such a manner, no matter what.

I think my time is nearly up, as *Skylark* manages this link, not I... so, until we meet again, I hope that your pathway is as fulfilling as mine.

With the greatest of respect,
Diana.

ALAN RICKMAN

A BIT OF A SURPRISE, BUT I GOT THERE!
(13/10/17 - 11:56)

When I walked through the valley of the shadow of death, I expected nothing... absolutely nothing! If I hadn't been sent absent healing, I might never be speaking to you now. I thought I would go into infinity, as the scriptures had little meaning to me. The 'infinity' I speak of is where I would be part of the emptiness of beyond. Mediums and astrology didn't enter my vocabulary, along with astronomy or the wonders of the universe. Now though, it is different, as my friend Patrick Moore has explained so many things, when we look at the moon together. Still, the enthusiasm for the moon runs in his veins. It will always be with him, just as Professor Snape is with me. I explained something to *Skylark* once about him, and when she next watched the films and got to the final one, she wept at what she witnessed. *'What was that'* you may think, and *'is she soft?'*

Love can make you like that, and it was love which I spoke about. It would be easy to dismiss Snape as a bit of a character, and not that pleasant. Yet, love is at the heart of him, through and through. It is love that made him look after Harry, and give his life, as he knew what was coming. Yet at the end, when he looked at Harry, he saw only love in and on his face. He saw Lily, and knew that he must, even as he lay dying, help her son. Lily never left him; she was always in his heart. So, his life may be seen as one where love was uppermost, even if it had died; as part of him died when she did.

Professor Snape is one of my favourite roles that I have ever played, because of the depth it required. I never accepted it for prestige or money, although the financial side would always be welcome, in any role that I undertook. I wanted to play Severus because I knew I could do it, and show love. It is there, and if you watch these films again, you will see differently the man at the head of Slytherin.

I had love in my life in so many ways, as a man and partner, and with the friends I have. I say 'have,' as it does not mean that because I

am no longer with them in physical form, that I cannot still love them…
I do with every fibre of my being, and I vibrate with the joy of it.

*****

DAVID BOWIE

A NEW NAME AND A NEW ROLE TO PLAY?
(13/10/17 - 14.55)

I thought I was in a drug-fuelled dream! I looked around, and couldn't believe what I was seeing. I thought that the end had well and truly come, or else I was on one massive trip; caused by what was going on around me. I actually like the idea of not being aware of my surroundings, which is a little selfish of me; but that's how I sometimes was... or had been. Never, I hope, to my wife... my soul mate of the truest and best kind. You know, Iman realises she is not alone, as do one or two of my friends, but they daren't believe, or can't accept what they are seeing and feeling. Well, it's me... so don't doubt it!

When I was in my early days of music, I was a git with an ego... there, I've said it... and I mean it! I feel a bit embarrassed about that now, and with all the fan stuff after I died. I am human, and no immortal! If I had been an influence on people's lives, I wish it was for something else.

Rose will be a big one, and will really go for it: I wish her all the best, as I doubt it will be easy. It never is, if you take on presidents and corporations... and she will! I want to make clear that I don't regret my music... none of it... but I can see that if I wanted to make an impact, then maybe I should have gone about it differently. Hindsight is wonderful!

I have never been loquacious, prattling away for hours on end... I never could stand it if people did; but I have met again the greatest of guys who does this, and I love him for it. It was a challenge at first, as I thought he just went on and on and on, and it took some getting used to. Now I don't mind, and would miss him if he went away. We play music together, and experiment with our sound and vision in the Halls of Music, along with a few others. I never thought I would say this, but Freddie Mercury is one of the most talented guys, in music, I have come across in a long time... yet can he talk! He will talk to anybody, and that's what makes him so great, because he is helping them at the same time.

I am cured of all my bodily afflictions, so my eyes are clear and my vision bright. I don't need glasses unless I choose to wear them. Seeing that I don't choose to, I don't bother, and my eyes are the best they have ever been. It's like that with everything, for all of us, so we can show ourselves fit and well, if ever a family member dreams about us. Dreams are one way we can be close to our family, but not as a nightly occurrence, as it might hack off even the most loving and tolerant of spouses.

You know, *Skylark* has painted me in etheric form for her friend Tilly, who saw me in concert years ago. It's nothing to get excited about, but I am excited about Vincent coming through to paint with her… Van Gogh that is! He has helped her already, but if *Skylark* doesn't mind me saying, there is a long way to go yet. The pathway is like that, step by step by step, and I am learning about it.

I have sat in Isaiah Abbotsbury's development circle, from spirit side. It's interesting to a newbie like me to learn about automatic writing, channelling your guide, and the difference between spiritual and intuitive linking. I also like him, his wife Tilly and *Skylark*, and I am not afraid to say so. They are not dramatic, yet like a good time, and enjoy it when they sit together for development. I think that's how it should be, but I am a fine one to talk, as I liked nothing more than a bit of drama, when I got going.

I want to finish with a personal message: '*Roses are red, violets are blue, I know that my love will always be true*'.

Love you forever,
David

ROBIN WILIAMS

A ROBIN WITH A SONG TO SING
(21/10/17 - 11:45)

Boy, do I have a few songs to sing to all of you! I love my life in heaven. I want to call it this, because that is what it feels like... so heavenly!

First of all, I want to say sorry to my family... you know why, without me having to go into details. It was a long time coming, and I love you all so much.

'GOOD MORNING VIETNAAAAAM' is often requested in the Halls of Rest, to wake folk up to where they are. I quite often have a few onlookers, which is great because it revs me up more. I love doing it, because I too have a new outlook on life. I also loved my genie role, despite the difficulties I had, and I love what I do now. Not easy at first, as you might understand, but a counsellor in the Halls of Rest helped me, more than you can ever realise. I see so much clearer now, about my life and wellbeing. I want to thank her from the bottom of my heart for what she did, as it's made me who I am in heaven.

I would like to think that I am a helpful guy, and I get lots of opportunities to be one. Despite the wakeup call, which I am asked to do, I also talk to a lot of people, with such freedom of soul, that it makes me want to do even more. It's like that here; the more you do, the more you want to. We all have the same inspiration, and that is the wonderful guy called God... one heck of a man, if I may say so, and I respect him a lot. He spoke to me... **WHAT**... yep, he did! I was able to ask him about the Earth, and all the grumpy and greedy people I had met. He said that it was just how it is, but that things will change, because he is going to make sure they do... as Rose is just for starters.

Don't think that God is talking about vengeance because he is not, and if you have got the message so far, you will know that. If you throw acid, that's a different story, but then you get what's coming... in the karmic, way that is. So, it makes sense to try to be nice; as being

60

nice doesn't mean that you are a pushover… it just feels nicer to be an okay guy, than a grumpy one. I should know, as I have experienced serious grumpiness. I kind of feel that what I experienced is going to help me, as I try to explain to other people about the 'why' of my life. People ask, and I am not afraid any more of talking from my heart, as I am not expected to perform (only when I do the *'you know what'* in the H of R… and I don't mind that).

I like being asked to do stuff because I am 'me,' and not a comedian or Hollywood actor; that's all in the past, as far as I am concerned. So, what I do from here on in is important, because it's going to inform and enlighten not only me, but others. I met Elvis not so long ago and we got talking. I wanted to ask him stuff, but I held back; as I felt that if he wanted to, he would open up and talk to me about a lot of things. I didn't go barging in, which is the opposite of what I had to deal with sometimes. I am learning to sing my *'song of life',* and it feels good.

So, until we meet again, remember that what we do goes around, and can smack us in the face, if we are not careful. So, when you go doing things that aren't good, life has a way of giving it back tenfold… and if it doesn't in this lifetime, it will in the next.

*****

FREDDIE MERCURY

A NEW TUNE AND A NEW SONG OR TWO
(21/10/17 - 12:25)

I don't look back in anger, but I do look back and think, *oh Freddie why did you behave in such a way?* At the time I was expressing my sexuality, in the way I enjoyed and wanted to. Now I know that my lovely guide Samuel shared those times with me, I could squirm in embarrassment. He took it all in his stride and never judged me one bit. I love him for the way he spoke, with no recrimination whatsoever.

Sam said that we have to look at my life, because of my karma, and I said 'okay.' So we looked at a lot, and he said to me that people loved me, but not everybody 'got' me. No judgement in those words, and I could see what he meant. I had hangers-on, but I also see with clarity those who loved and accepted me, and I wish I could have spent more time with them. Who knows, in the scheme of things, what will happen in life? Maybe I might get the chance to say 'hi' and 'I love and admire you, for simply being the great person you are.' I wish I'd had that said to me, but at least, in the appropriate way, I can say this to my friends... or at least one in particular. It is karmically imprinted, but there is always freewill involved, and I am learning a lot about that one.

I thought I might be 'in for it' with God - you know, all that Old Testament stuff - but I was not. After my experience with Sam, and looking at my life, I knew God would be like him. I did ask about the stuff written in the Bible (*Leviticus 18:22, 19:*31), as *Skylark* could be seen as coming under that judgement too. It hasn't put her off walking her pathway. She knows that she is not like the seer's and mediums back then, and has no judgement from any in spirit for what she does... in fact it is the opposite... and the same for Isaiah Abbotsbury, a man whom I admire greatly. So, it is the same for all of us from the LGBT community. We are loved in heaven for who we are, and not judged for our same sex relationships... and I say 'hurray' and about time you all know that. I hope it helps, but it is my experience we are talking about, and I have received no ill will from anybody I have spoken to.

One of the great joys about life here is that we are free to go where we wish, and I have met some amazing people. You can't just barge up to them, as you have to ask their permission first. I like that, as then you meet as equals. It also means that if you had a serious problem with anyone, they can't continue it once they have passed over. Bullying is not allowed. These kinds of people are segregated until they heal and learn differently, so they can't hassle or intimidate, or do deals behind the backs of their guides.

We all have guides in spirit, who try to teach and encourage us to explore and learn in the Halls of Learning... or in my case, the Halls of Music. I didn't need much encouraging, and I was really keen to meet up with John Lennon and David Bowie, with whom I also paint, under the watchful eye of our friend and mentor Vincent. I think I got to David at the start, with all my talking, but he took it in his stride and we spend a lot of time together now. Would it surprise you if I said that he does some teaching in the Halls of Music? A lot of us do, and that's before I get onto the likes of Mozart.

I am constantly busy, but you don't have to be; you can be as idle and lazy as you like, yet the energy here uplifts and enhances your vibration, so you don't want to be. It's good, really good, and I can't begin to exaggerate the lightness of heart and mind, which benefits us, if we let it. God has thought about so much to bring joy, and if only you knew, then the doctrinal aspects of the varying churches would allow for so much freedom, and not fear of judgement. The pews would be fuller then, in my opinion. Still, I didn't mean to preach, and never wanted to, as I couldn't stand it myself... and it probably surprises you. You get to see things differently sometimes - after time and experience - and that is one of them.

*****

ELVIS PRESLEY

A DIFFERENT GRACELAND
(03/11/17 - 11:50)

My favourite hymn is the amazing 'How Great Thou Art'. I love it, and still like to sing it with emotion. I am a lot more in tune with myself than what I was in my life as Elvis Presley... a lot more... and now understand why I ate like I did. Food brought me comfort, and when I was young I vowed to myself that I would never go hungry again. I didn't, but it was a heavy price to pay.

My cook was marvellous, and she knew what I liked. In her way she loved me, and that was how she showed it. It may have done me no favours, but few refused me what I asked, and maybe they should have. Still, I could threaten and use my money as a tool to get what I wanted, but I hope I wasn't a bad man. I did try to do my best, but I felt emotional about one or two things, and food was one of them. I hope I am remembered for my songs, and not my weight; as that is a better testament to my life's work of singing my heart out.

Many people think they have seen me, and I was even thought to be in a town in Leicestershire once, many years ago... but I wasn't. Also, a lot have tried to impersonate me, and I don't mind, as it means that my songs still live and bring pleasure. I don't mind a lot of things now, which used to get to me. I have no money, and don't need it... and that, after all I went through as a boy, is the most important thing to me. They say you can't take it with you and you really can't, as money doesn't talk in these hallowed halls... which is a good thing, as then it loses its power, and control over the human soul.

I saw when I got here how I used my money. Sometimes for good, and quite often I liked being able to do what I wanted, at a moment's notice, because I could, quite simply. I am not like that now, as I have had a whole load of help to get me on the straight and narrow, from a lovely lady called Rebecca, in the Halls of Rest. She told me what I needed to hear and showed me what I ought to see. It was difficult, but I have seen the light and I say 'hallelujah' for that. Rebecca did me one

64

of the best things by doing that, as I was still hung-up on food and the cocktails of what I was used to. Now I am light and nimble and I sing with joy in my heart. It is not a chore or must that I do it... I want to, because I can see what happiness it brings to other people, and the joy I feel when I sing. It makes me want to go the extra mile.

I don't need the trappings of the life I had, and I'd like to say thank you to the *'man in the sky'* for that. One big difference though, is that he isn't in the sky, but in my heart, in the truest and best way. That's why I say that 'How Great Thou Art' is one of my favourites, because God is one of the greatest miracles of my life.

*****

IAN FLEMING

007
(03/11/17 - 12:28)

…That's not quite how I think of myself, but I did have a few experiences I used in my writings, which weren't that different to what *007* had. It's not often I have the honour to dictate to a lovely lady, and I like the idea of being able to have the opportunity.

I know *Skylark* far better than any of you, as it's not my first time of writing. Most of us have penned the odd letter, when asked to by her guides, and it's always a pleasure to help a lady out. We have met formally in spirit, so I am not a complete stranger, even if it feels like it to her. That's how it should be, as we all have to behave in appropriate ways. If we didn't, either *Skylark* or her doorkeeper, Matthias, would show us the door. Matthias is no softie, yet he is a perfect gentleman… a bit like me really, except I am not a vastly experienced spirit plane guide, like he is. If he was near any of my Bond villains, they would take one look and scarper… quick! He knows *Skylark* very well, as they have shared a lot of lives as student and guide… even going back to the Egypt of the pharaohs. My guide is a lovely man called Daniel. I hope to have the honour of him also being so in a future life, as he has a lot to teach me.

So, what am I going to say… or am I going to blag it? I could do that easily, as I still have that skill-set with me from Earth. I got up to a few shenanigans in my time, that's why I could write my books. I also listened a lot, and intently, so I could mould some of what I heard into my Bond, or the situations he got into. Never plagiarism, so don't think it, but a writer will watch and hear the nuances around him or her, and take inspiration from life… and that's what I did. I am not alone, as I know a man a bit like me, writing away, using his life to fuel the books he writes. Ask Isaiah Abbotsbury about him, as he knows him too. Nothing like a bit of a plug. We do this in spirit; help each other out when the need arises.

Queen and country was a focus in my life. I may have moved

66

away from *"Blighty"* at one stage, but I never forgot what home was like. It was hot where I lived, but not like the heat and storms you get now. We sent a lot of healing, to help after the hurricanes… it was sad to see people with their homes destroyed. We can't rebuild homes, but we can send absent healing to help fortify the soul. We shall always do so when times require it, but you have to look after the planet better, and then she will treat you with respect. It makes sense if you think about it, as nobody likes to be dumped on, so why should this planet of ours be? The will has to be there… but is it? Or do you think *'nothing to do with me?'* Well, it's actually to do with all of us! I shall reincarnate, and I want something green and pleasant, and not dry and parched, with mountains of rubbish… literally so! None of us can be *'I'm alright Jack,'* that no longer has any role to play in the lives we shall reincarnate into. You all will, and mine is coming up fairly soon, so I might be luckier than some of you… then again, I might not… as it won't be my last!

*****

ARTHUR CONAN DOYLE

NO NAME IS BETTER THAN NONE
(14/11/17 - 15:40)

That is just the kind of problem 'my' Sherlock Holmes would have enjoyed: the meaning of the name of the letter. It would have given him some time to think, which is what he liked to do. Sherlock liked mental stimulation, as his character was flawed and he was uncomfortable with himself. That is why; whenever he was bored he would go off-the-rails, and behave in ways that made Watson concerned.

What do I think of all the Sherlocks, since first I put pen to paper? Little, if I am honest! That is not meant as an insult, but I wish I had dealt with things differently, so there was less improvisation and room for manoeuvre. I did not, so I have to suffer the consequences of my lack of thought.

I did not foresee such a monstrosity as a television set, in the development of the human intellect and desire for entertainment. If I had seen it on the horizon then maybe, just maybe, I could have been more prepared for the potential of future Sherlock Holmes. The one I like and admire the best I will not say, but *Skylark* and I are in agreement and she has enough tact not to say which one. I may be a man of few words and brusque, but I would not willingly wish to upset anyone, as all of the adaptations have involved decent men and women, and a lot of hard work. At least though, I have been able to say something on the subject, and for that I am grateful.

You will have another writer, later on, with a different approach to the subject of solving puzzles, clues and trapping villains. I happen to like and admire Margery Allingham and her approach to her work, so I wish her all the best with her letter.

*****

FLORENCE NIGHTINGALE

WHAT GOOD COMES FROM WAR?
(14/11/17 - 16:04)

I speak of my experiences in the Crimean, as the men in the British Army suffered enormously, at the hands of incompetent surgeons and generals. Their other officers were not much better! I was insulted more than once, by a doctor intent on invasive surgery, when I suggested different. My memories of the time I spent in the hospital - if it could be called that - are crystal clear, and history has misconstrued one or two things, which I want to put straight.

1.   Mary Seacole is a woman to admire. I do admire her and we work closely together in the Halls of Rest. Maybe I was not altogether clear in what I felt at the time, as she was different to what I was used to, but I was grateful to her for the good she did and still am.

2.   I cannot exaggerate the histrionics of some of the doctors when we arrived. Unwanted and unwelcomed, and thought to be meddling in affairs that were of no concern of ours. Not all were like that fortunately, but it was still difficult.

3.   No matter what, I tried to do my best under the conditions forced upon me. I was no saint, and the moniker given to me could have applied to a lot of my nurses. I cannot take credit unless it is due, and the nurses with me were determined to help the men. Such was their compassion that on occasion's men would cry out that we were angels. 'No' I say to that, but sometimes amidst the stench and squalor, I felt that 'yes,' we had a guiding hand from the almighty, as he was then called.

Nowadays nursing is different, but no easier, for all its steps forward in pain relief and hygiene. I visit the wards often. I see the overworked doctors and nurses trying their best; understaffed, with little time for even the basics, on some occasions. The National Health Service of the United Kingdom is a marvellous gift to its people. I applaud its creation, and wish that it was not taken advantage of so much, through lack of understanding and abusive behaviour towards its staff. Yet, *Skylark* has benefitted from the care of a good doctor and nurse in the casualty department where she lives. They went beyond what was necessary, and I thank them for it, as someone has to.

The doctors, nurses, paramedics, and technicians of the National Health Service are a credit to the country. They often have to work in stressed conditions, with little care for how *they are*.

I, Florence Nightingale, would like to say 'thank you' to you... thank you for your generosity of heart and soul, for the kindnesses you give to those in your care, and remember that you are valued far more than what you realise.

*****

(MOTHER) TERESA

I WAS NO SAINT
(15/11/17 - 11:50)

When I died, I thought I was in heaven, yet it felt odd; almost surreal. I wanted to be with Jesus, and hoped I would be, but it was not what I expected. It was better than I ever could have hoped for. I felt the arms of love surround me, and knew I had gone to be with my Lord. Oh, how I wish I could truthfully say this to you… to say it was better than I could ever have hoped for, means that I had an expectation. Don't we all? Or do some of you, like Alan earlier, think it's the sleep we never wake up from? *The nothingness beyond the grave,* which is what I have heard more than once. But, I say, the dream of peace can become a reality, and *nothing* can become *something* if the chance is given.

I hoped and dreamed that I would be with Jesus, as I sometimes felt he was with me, and I did not want this to stop. Maybe it was arrogant of me to think that I should go to heaven, or that I was good enough. But, my friends, heaven doesn't require anything of us and nor does God. In the Old Testament book of Micah (*6:8*) we find a verse about what God would like from us. Sometimes, I would reflect on this, but I knew in my dealings with people that I couldn't be a fool, with eyes that were half closed. I had to be far from 'other worldly,' if I were to achieve what I privately wished and hoped for. Yet, I *wanted* to set an example that would inspire my sisters, and give hope to the dying. I *wanted* none to die lonely and unloved, and I hope that I did my best to do this. As a nun I can have no 'wants,' but I was determined to do my utmost for the poor and outcast of where I lived… I felt that 'wanted' was a word of determination I would inwardly use.

My prayers to God were always for the outcast. I thought *that was how Jesus lived, as he himself was cast out at birth, and forced to flee with no home to go to.* The reality of his birth and life is different to what I previously knew and was taught. I was challenged in heaven by truths I never expected. Challenged by the idea that the power of the cross has a new and different metaphysical understanding, beyond what I had previously imagined it to be. What I had understood to be infallible

71

was on occasions nothing more than fiction. A means to show that Jesus was who *'the word'* said he was. Yet, I have taken to my new understanding with joy in my heart and I feel free: not bound by what I thought would land me in hell. Free to be 'me,' and I love and thank God for this. I do not have to follow or toe the line of any church or organisation, and I cry with the joy of being able to question. Yes, question what I consider to be misleading and feel no retribution or scandal because of it. God wants me to ask, so he can bring love even closer to me. I am empowered by his love, to keep on asking and wishing to learn more and more.

Life is beautiful, friends… so beautiful! *Skylark* knows this from the healing she receives. Yesterday I sent absent healing to *Skylark,* and I am so grateful that she felt the benefit of it. It didn't prevent or stop the karma of her journey's experience, but it gave her the ability to do what she wished to at the time. Love is like this, friends… it gives us wings with which to fly, and always with freedom of choice.

*****

BENEDICT

…NEITHER WAS I
(24/11/17 - 10:50)

I am thought to be a saint, and head of a group of people passionate about their faith and hospitality to visitors. I would always applaud the gift of a gracious host: given with love and no thought of what they could gain from it. *Skylark* herself has been on retreat at Worth Abbey, and felt it was a warm and comfortable place; with a dining room for visitors far beyond her expectations. But it was not for her. By the time Sunday had arrived and a good few church services had been attended, her love of God was still intact, but she was glazing over during the services. Not a surprise, as I felt like that sometimes. I tried my best and wanted to love God, but I didn't find it an easy journey to begin with. By the time I was close to death, I thought I had learnt a lot and had given a rule to help monks find their path in community. Now I think differently!

Community… well, what is it… a group of people finding how to get on with each other, so that each day flows with love and goodness? Or is it a means of control? I am open to suggestion on that one. When men or women live together in a large band of mixed backgrounds, there needs to be a common ground, so that all know what the boundaries are. Should that also include celibacy, if it is monks showing their love for each other and God, by stepping away from the world and into prayer? Yet, a lot of nuns and monks are in the world, in a vital and important way, so why should they not be allowed to have what others have… and that is a family, with a wife or husband to come home to.

A friend of *Skylark's* once said, that a Benedictine she knew thought of her and the other people who helped him as his family. He was right in this, as they loved him; but I could see that his love was so generous, he could still have been a husband and father, and it would not have detracted him from his ministry. Is the Church of England wrong to have a female bishop, or even to have ordained women? I say 'no,' they were not wrong! Women ministered to Jesus and for him, and they have a lot to offer, in that way, now.

I would also like to say something a little controversial, but I know *Skylark* agrees with me, as I recently heard her say something similar. I do not think Paul wrote the letters attributed to him in the New Testament. I know Paul, and the man I know would have welcomed all into the fold of God, and not expected silence as part of the bargain. I say 'bargain,' as in some ways women have had to do this over the history of the world… keep silent in case of bringing offence, thought to be stupid, or even endangering themselves. The bargain is what they have to give up when they do speak their minds, or see a different point of view. I have never thought of myself as a feminist, but I cannot stand by when I see inequality on the road to salvation. This path is one of opportunities, given freely by God, so that means every single person, regardless of gender or sexual orientation should be treated equally. They are in heaven, as one of the most skilled guides *Skylark* has is a nun called Rachel. A bright soul indeed, and generous to a fault, yet Rachel is no fool, nor has she ever been treated as one.

Her journey has been a long one. She was supported by God, as she trod her path, life by life. No one ever said that she could not do it, because she was a woman. Rose though, who spoke earlier, has to reincarnate as a man, in order for her voice to heard and taken seriously. What does that tell you? I know what it says to me, *that we have some way to go in the evolution of the world, and the respect we give to each other.* Yet, I know some of the plans heaven has, to help you all, which go beyond what Rose has to say.

As the books unfold, so communicators will speak about different things, and you will know just how much you are valued and loved.

For now, I leave the love of heaven with you on your road to enlightenment. May it be one filled with love and opportunities. All you have to do is ask, and the door will be opened.

God bless.

HENRY (the EIGHTH of that name)

MY LEGACY IS DIFFERENT TO WHAT I HOPED
IT WOULD BE
(24/11/17 - 12:33)

I did not want to be known as a king who mistreated his wives, or as a tyrant, whose court was full of intrigue and jostling for position. I am remembered for both, and the execution of two wives, who never should have been treated in such a way! I missed Anne Boleyn after she died, but could say nothing. Inside my heart I was aware of the pain I felt, and the shallowness of my soul. I couldn't admit it though. Never. I, the great and glorious Henry - couldn't say I was wrong - so I went from wife to wife and blamed everybody but myself. I did get to like Anne of Cleves though, after time went by, but never as my queen, as she wasn't my 'cup of tea,' as they say.

I blamed anybody and everybody when I felt like it, and enjoyed it when they scuttled about like insects, trying to do my bidding. I was surrounded by the biggest group of toady nobles, all trying to get into my good books; killing each other in the process, if they had to. Setting one and another up for a fall, only to find they were next. Perhaps I am being hard on myself, as I hope that history sees some good in my reign, and that of my children's.

My family's lives are quite well documented, but you do not know everything, so there is more to tell. Some things are best left unsaid, but I cannot dictate any longer, so I have to leave what each say up to them. I know a little so, expect a surprise from my son Edward… and, always will I think of him as such!

We Tudors are a strange bunch. My grandmother Margaret - or so I was told - was a vengeful woman, with the utmost patience… not surprising really! My father had no respect for her, which is far from how records portray it. He kept her close by his side, as he new she would serve him well… and she did! She got him to where he wanted to be… simple as that! Neither did he like my mother, but she had a purpose too. He had her watched, to detect for signs of intrigue. Once she bore a son things changed, and I think he began to tolerate the woman, who could unite a kingdom. I don't know if he ever trusted anyone. I felt his coolness and mistrust from afar. I thought he even had me spied on, as there were too many things I couldn't explain, which he spoke of or wrote about. I suppose that was no surprise, as it took murder and double-dealing to get him on the throne.

It's different now, as he is willing to learn; unlike before when he lingered by himself, refusing to see or listen to what his guides said to him. He is not yet a reformed man, but he is open and ready to explore some of what his karma offers him... so he is making progress and going the right way. Not this book, but in another, you will read the flavour of the man, as he is ready to talk about his life and ambitions. His guide will be with him, so *Skylark* need have no worries there.

Skylark understands how the linking works, as Richard, who preceded my father, has already told her one or two things in the first draft of this book; so she knows the format and manages things accordingly.

What else can I say to you all? Probably a lot, but as I am not as full of bluster, as I used to be, I will keep it simple... I desperately wanted and needed an heir, but I know inside of me, that if Anne Boleyn had remained my wife, I would have been a much, much, happier man.

Henry

ANNE BOLEYN

TOO LITTLE... TOO LATE
(24/11/17 - 15:55)

I told Henry, when he came snivelling to me in the spirit plane, that it was too little and too late... and no matter how much he cried, I wanted nothing to do with him. I am not a bitter or sour woman, but when you are lied about and your family destroyed, it is a difficult thing to forgive. I have healed of a lot and I can forgive him now, but that forgiveness does not include us being husband and wife once more. He has said his piece and I have said mine.

Henry is a changed man; no longer the strutting peacock of his youth, but we have one thing we agree on, and that is our daughter Elizabeth. My Elizabeth; whom I love with all my heart and soul. Of course Henry is proud, as she is the great Gloriana... the woman who was king. A child to be proud of and we both are! Did you know that Elizabeth cried when she saw me in spirit? She called me 'mama' and my heart wept, with the sound of her voice saying those words. We are close as mother and daughter would be, and I like to think that she loves me as I love her.

I have a different life to Queen of England, and it is one that I love and enjoy more. If you were to see me, you would notice a ginger cat or two by my side. I never go anywhere without them, and they are my joy. I teach healing in the Halls of Rest, with my guide Simon. Still, there are questions about my life, and on occasions, with Simon close by, I will give a question and answer session. There is the odd historian or researcher, with a keen eye, who has noticed a discrepancy in a document, or who has the simplest of questions, which requires a full answer... which I give to the best of my ability. I don't mind giving help when asked, if it will clarify an issue.

There is something you may not expect me to say, but I felt for Catherine Howard; married to a man she should never have called husband. She vomited when alone, as she finally understood the enormity of marriage to a man old enough to be her father. Henry was overweight, irritable, and ill. He thought Catherine would bring his youth back. She did not, and she paid the price for that, and her foolishness. I do not blame her for seeking comfort, but it was a dangerous thing to do, when married to a king like Henry.

He should have stayed with Anne of Cleves. She was a wise bird that one. Knew what to say to keep her head, and remain on friendly terms... with a good pay-out to boot! Anne and I get on well, and she was kind to Elizabeth... I am grateful for that!

History has not told my full story, and how can it...? As there are the quiet, private moments of joy, and the fear I felt as I walked to my death. I would be willing to say more, but I cannot be greedy and take advantage of *Skylark's* generosity... so, until you read my other letters, I wish you adieu.

*****

ANNE OF CLEVES

HE SHOULD HAVE BEEN GRATEFUL
(25/11/17 - 11:20)

When I first laid eyes on Henry, I thought, *what have I let myself in for?* He was as disgusting as I had been told, and he stank like a farmyard. He should have been grateful to have a queen like me, and not moaned about how I was not comely to him.

Before I went to England, I spoke with my family, as I did not want to end up like (my dear friend) Anne Boleyn. My brother said, at the first sign of trouble he would get me out, so I went under this assurance. What I was also supposed to do was gather information and feed this back to him. He didn't trust Henry, so it was the perfect ruse to look like a loyal queen at the same time. I would have made a marvellous secret agent, and I think I could have rivalled James Bond, if he were a real character. Perhaps that is my ego speaking, but at the time, I think I made quite a good job of it!

After annulment, my brother said to remain, as I could continue my profession. I wasn't unhappy about that; I was pleased with my pay-off, as it was more than I had ever had. I had to be discreet about one or two things, as I was not an old woman and had my desires; so discretion was paramount for my own safety. Henry may not have wanted me, but his ego was such that no one else could; so I had to be discreet. Aided by trusted servants, and the dead of night... perhaps Ian (Fleming) could have used that in one of his books... or has he?

I may as well get it all off my chest while I am at it, but Henry was impotent and it was none of my doing! What do you expect of a man in his condition? In a lot of ways I was not sorry to be queen. Imagine having to say goodnight, I shudder at the thought of it. Poor Catherine Howard... like Anne Boleyn, I felt so sorry for her... a chit of a girl, and a bit silly in the poisonous atmosphere of the court. Poor child she never really stood a chance. I prayed for her and why not? I may have been wife number four, and she five after me, but I held no ill will towards her. She needed all the help she could get, so I included her in my prayers, along with myself.

Even though I could not be easily disposed of, it had been a bit tricky to begin with. I had to have my wits about me, to avoid offending the royal ego, and not be a challenge to the Duke of Norfolk.

I also felt sorry for Cromwell… you could tell that time was running out, and what Henry did was cruel at the end. You know Henry blubbed like a baby in front of me, ruing the day he had Cromwell executed, as nobody else understood him like he did… Phah! Did he really expect me to feel sorry for him, blubbering away and blaming everybody else for his own actions? I even began to wonder if he was turning into an idiot… but no… just a buffoon!

Skylark has wondered what happened to Anne Boleyn's family after she died… I can tell you one thing about that… I was very fond of Elizabeth… very fond indeed! I thought her a bright girl; intelligent and witty. I couldn't do a lot for her, but decided to be kind whenever possible; as I felt that would go a long way.

As for Mary, her sister… she was odd! I didn't see much of her, but I heard bits and pieces, and wondered if she was insane. She loved her mother, and Henry was unkind in the way he kept them apart. What Catherine and Mary wanted was to spend their days with each other. No wonder Mary ended up like she did! When Henry went to spirit, he understood a lot more about his life, and cried over his children. I can't say more than that, as it's up to them… but he, at last, began to see that he was no father. Mind you, with the one he had, it's not surprising!

I want you all to understand that I am not a bitter woman. Why should I be, as I had a lucky escape and was financially secure. I witnessed quite a bit, and heard things, but I am not as emotionally involved as some of the others in Henry's life. I can talk about what I saw, but you have to make your own minds up about what I say.

I shall sign off now, and hand over to wife number five.

With the best of wishes,
Anne of Cleves

CATHERINE HOWARD

I LIVED IN FEAR
(25/11/17 - 12:25)

Before I became queen I was a gay girl… always cheerful! I thought myself pretty; perhaps not beautiful, but comely enough. I felt flattered when I was told I would be dangled in front of the king, like a ripe piece of fruit. I heard rumours that Henry stank like a pig, with bad breath. My uncle Norfolk had said as much to my parents, but I didn't dwell on it, as most people I knew had some sort of personal odour, and one or two had lice. So, I ended up being married to a man who murdered me!

It was foolish to behave as I did. I was desperate for some sort of comfort, as I had none from the man I married… or not the sort I craved. I could never have had a child, as Henry could not father one. So, when I was executed, the child I was carrying was not his, but my lover's. We are together in spirit - my son and I - and he looks very much like me. I said nothing at the time, as I did not want any to know, as it would only inflame matters more. If I was going to die, then I wished to as a queen, and not as one accused of treason.

On our wedding evening, I was caught up with the thrill and excitement of our marriage. In the morning, and in privacy, I retched and vomited like I had never done before. I regretted listening to my family, yet at the same time, needed little persuading. So, I behaved without reason when I took a lover, and hoped we could get away with it. Fool that I was! How on Earth I thought it possible, I do not know!

So, here I am, writing as wife number five, and remembered as being another queen executed by Henry the Eighth. That is only one of the lives I have lived; others have been far more enjoyable and fulfilling. I am due to reincarnate soon, so it is good for me to say now what I wish to… I am looking forward to my next life, as I will explore the metaphysical and esoteric, and learn about the healing energy. I look forward to it a lot. As for me and Henry? It's done… I no longer have anything to do with him. I listened to his words of sorrow at what happed, and then basically told him to go away, in no uncertain terms. I never forgave him for a long time, as I thought he could sit and stew in it. When I asked to speak to him once more, I told him what I thought and finally gave the forgiveness he craved. It benefitted me emotionally to do this… far more so than I thought it would. I had let go of the past and moved forward, ready to explore what my karma offered. I liked that very much, as I felt so free and weightless - not burdened by my emotions. So until or if ever, our paths cross again… goodbye, with no regrets, from me, a queen, who would like to be forgotten.

*****

EDWARD (the SIXTH of that name)

I WOULD HAVE BEEN WORSE THAN MY SISTER, MARY
(24/11/17 - 15:25)

The title of my letter is truthful... I was a priggish boy; full of my own importance, and fanatical about the new Protestant faith. No popery in my kingdom, if I had my way... and I would have had my people executed for their beliefs. So, I am not that far from Mary, except for one thing... I am not my father's son!

When I originally told *Skylark* this, she was wide eyed in disbelief, with a great big **'NO!'** I was excited to tell her, and she felt my emotion... she wondered what it was that I was going to say.

Now you all know, the great Henry of England did not have a royal son. My uncles persuaded a distant cousin to do what was needed. I came along and was passed off as Henry's son and heir. From what I have been told, it took some planning and my mother was willing, as she knew the favour it would bring. It was a risk my family thought was worth taking, and to some extent it paid off. None of them expected my mother to die, and afterwards the cousin was heard of no more. How has this changed history? The kingdom even? 'I don't know' is the answer to that as I still had two sisters.

Anne Boleyn may yet have had a son, if she had not been executed... and that would have changed everything. Still, I have wondered... and then again, it is what it is... and that's the lie of the land! Perhaps it's also for the best, that I did not live to be an elderly king, as maybe my reputation would have been worse than that of my sister, Mary Tudor. Then again, the Stuarts which followed us were an odd bunch, and they ended up dividing the kingdom. So, the Tudors and Stuarts left a legacy to fill your books, and inform your evenings with documentaries... what more can I say?

(This is the order in which Henry's family came through so I don't quite know how I managed to get the date incorrect, sorry about that - Skylark)

ELIZABETH (the FIRST of that name)

I WAS ONLY A GIRL WHEN I BECAME QUEEN
(25/11/17 - 15:08)

That's what I like to think, but I had prepared for this day for a very long time. When I knew how the land lay, and that my sister would never have a child, I was secretly pleased. I would be safe - I thought - as queen, but I knew it was not a foregone conclusion. I still had to be careful, as Mary was a queen with a purpose, and I was part of that. I was a Protestant. She dare not kill me… and I think in her heart, she did not want to. I was thought to be her flesh and blood, when it came down to it… she knew that, and would behave properly no matter what.

Her husband Philip was an ungracious man, who used her. *Poor Mary!* I often thought her father didn't want us, and her mother so desperately wished to be with her… and Mary likewise. I had no choice. I wished for a mother, only to find out that papa (as I thought of him) had her beheaded. That was a shock, and at first I couldn't believe it. I vowed after, that no man would ever rule me if I became queen… and none ever did!

When I went to spirit, I saw my mother, and my heart so filled with love that I cried and cried. All I could say was her name… and when I said 'mama' it felt like heaven had opened and poured its bounty on me. We both cried, and are rarely parted now. I like that, so much so that our guides say that even in death we are like one!

Death is an illusion, as it is the physical body and not the spirit… so if I can be with my mama, then all of us can be with the ones we love. I never loved any man when I was queen… not even Dudley or Essex. I liked to flirt and behave coquettishly, but as for physical love… no, not for me! Even in pleasure I did not want to be ruled.

There is one man who knew me through and through, and was loyal to the point of death. This man is Francis Walsingham, and he knows how to keep a secret or two… the same as Isaiah, Tilly, and *Skylark*. You can tell them a secret, and it is like saying nothing… I was like that too! *'Still waters run deep'* as the saying goes, and this applied to Francis. I didn't know just how much he did for me until I passed to spirit, and I would like to publicly say 'thank you' to him.

I didn't like all the members of my court or Privy Council, but they served me well. I felt sad when betrayed, and it ended in the Tower of London… few came out of there alive! When you entered you knew you were doomed, and hardly any were reprieved.

I am sorry for the deaths during my reign, except one… and that was the Duke of Norfolk. His ambition was too open… too easy to see! He was rude to me on occasions, and I couldn't have that, so I took the opportunity when it arose, to free me of his pestilence. *Good riddance* I privately thought, as I blamed his family for my mother and Catherine Howard. Naked ambition is a dangerous thing to have; mine was discreet. I had learnt the lessons of Henry's court well.

*****

FRANCIS WALSINGHAM

ALWAYS FOR QUEEN AND COUNTRY
(30/11/17 - 11:07)

This is not my first try at writing with *Skylark*. It is actually my third letter. She has reprimanded me via her doorkeeper Matthias, and this time I cannot step in with my 'spymaster hat' on my head. It was confusing for her, yet that is what I did, as I was working in my persona for that lifetime. So, it was a case of third try, and then I was out! Never to be written about, despite the secrets I have. So be it, as *Skylark* manages the link and not I. I should not have tried, as maybe I would have been lost to history, and known as just the man who helped safeguard a queen.

I loved Elizabeth. Always she was my focus, but I knew she would not love me in return. The right woman to be queen, or so I felt. She was wily and shrewd, and knew how to play the game; but could also be fair, and very much so. She didn't like the Cecils... father and son... neither did I! I wouldn't have trusted them with a barge pole... literally so, as Robert could be vicious, and his words could kill. He was a snake in the heart of that family, and vindictive, as we can see with regard to his persecution of John Gerard. Robert Cecil would never have given up, and if I am honest, neither would I, if Elizabeth had been at risk. Robert did it for ego, and he liked to manipulate. No matter who it was, he would try and rarely fail. His father had trained him well!

I walked a tricky path sometimes, and more than one wife wondered about my relationship with their husband, and what exactly it was. I would have done anything in the protection of my queen, and I liked to find out things. It was a personal challenge to get to the nub of it, but I don't think I was vindictive. I never perjured myself in front of a judge or jury... maybe to my fellow man, but not to God.

I wanted to know how the country faired when I first went to spirit. I was in isolation to begin with, but at one point I was given the opportunity to see how things were. I personally thought that James the Sixth was a dangerous man, and if I am honest, mentally unsound. I was looking from afar, I know that, yet could still see his instability and babbling.

So, what do I have to impart, other than my wily ways in gaining information? You may not believe what I am about to say, and it may not interest you, but Henry the Eighth was definitely cuckolded more than once by his wives. To their minds, it may have been to give him what he wanted more than anything, which was a son.

Mary Tudor - the queen with a legacy best left unsaid - was the only legitimate child of Henry's, who was his flesh and blood. Anne Boleyn would have you know that she was faithful to Henry, but she was aware that if she did not have a child who lived, then she was in danger. So, she did what she thought best, and Elizabeth was the consequence. I don't know how Anne managed it with the spies at court, but she did and none knew at the time. That means, how did I find out? My arm was long… and just as I was given a letter about Jane Seymour and her child, so evidence I suppressed was similar about Anne Boleyn. The men in these cases wrote it all down, to use if it ever came about… for their own protection and to seek favour. Yet both died and were never heard of, with their legacies left unsaid.

I did a similar thing…the man who gave me the documents about Elizabeth was not to be seen by another living soul… all for queen and country!

*****

ANNE OF DENMARK

I WAS FRIGHTENED BY THE IDIOT I WAS MARRIED TO, AND I HATED HIM WITH A VENGEANCE.
(02/12/17 - 11:57)

When I first laid eyes on my future husband, I wondered what I had let myself in for. It was thought to be a good match, as he could have sat on the throne of England. He did - as you all may know - but that doesn't make it any easier to tell a little of what marriage to him was like.

James, in the simplest way to describe was mentally unstable, and he brought an air of negativity with him wherever he went... which he enjoyed! He was obsessed with the occult, as many a book will say, but it was not healthy, as he behaved oddly at times; as though in conversation with another man. Sometimes he knew things and I don't know how. Of course, I thought he had me spied on, but then again what he came out with was private to me and others, so it can't have just been I alone under his gaze. He once joked that he had the best sneak in the world under his control, and laughed, saying that even Robert Cecil had no knowledge of his whereabouts. So, I don't know... but he was a very strange man indeed, with tastes to match.

You know, he lingers still in a world of his own, thinking he is king. The best and most experienced healer counselors are helping him, but it is a slow journey to health; for a man once thought to be of divine purpose. He never was - not to my mind anyway - as I had moments of privacy with him, where he would try to humiliate me in ways I cannot describe. Even then, I sometimes felt darkness in the room with us, and I would shudder at what I thought I saw.

When our son Henry died, he never forgave me and blamed me for his death. I never forgave him for taking Henry away, to be brought up by another. That was cruel... but then again, cruelty and cunning ran in his family. You only have to look at his mother for that. When she was executed, James showed no emotion, other than the way was clearer for him and he was pleased. No wonder at how he was treated and educated. Little love was ever shown to him, and his tastes reflected that. He could have been a fair man to Roman Catholics though, but never really had the opportunity to show this side to his nature. Sometimes I wondered if he liked to 'wind up' Robert Cecil, as he privately loathed the man, but saw his purpose and recognized the cunning in him.

I loved all my children, but I wonder if I ever knew them… certainly not Henry anyway. Charles maybe, but he was a sensitive child, with a sense of his own purpose in life. Henry - I hesitate to say, as he is my own flesh - I think could have been peevish, which isn't healthy for a king. You only have to look at the Tudors for that, especially Henry the Eighth. All those wives… I doubt any of them were truly happy. His pain made him vicious, and I am glad I was never his wife… but look who I was lumbered with!

I certainly didn't enjoy marriage, even if I was queen of a considerable nation, in the journals of history. I would have given up all the trappings to have peace of heart and soul. I have it now, and am so happy to be at one with life and love.

*****

CHARLES (the SECOND of that name)

LOCK UP YOUR WIVES AND DAUGHTERS
(02/12/17 - 12:48)

…Never has a truer word been written! I loved them all, but never behaved in a way that would have compromised my role as king. Pillow talk… well I knew the value of that, so I would not be trapped by any mistress, wishing to gain inside knowledge of my workings as king. I wouldn't have told a secret out of respect for my wife. If I wasn't able to tell the woman I was married to about this, that, and the other, then I most certainly would not have said anything to a whore, royal concubine, or another man's wife.

I did have someone I could talk to, and he was a man of mine, who I trusted very much… a servant of French origin, who was loyal to me and me only. I knew I could tell him my innermost thoughts, and he would say nothing. We talked together when I was alone. I would ask him to sit, so he was comfortable, take some wine, and then we would speak as men. I rarely mentioned my grandfather… the king by the name of James. My father… that was different… and how could it be any other? We spoke of him!

Papa did say one thing to me, a long time ago, which I found puzzling… he said that he always knew he would be king. How I asked? He replied, God had told him in a dream. Now, I doubt that God did anything of the sort, as I wasn't like my father; but we Stuarts are an odd bunch and I can't explain that away. He also said that he often thought his own father was a little peculiar, because he would talk and laugh out loud, when he didn't appear to be in conversation with another living soul. After what my grandmother has just said, I am not surprised at anything!

I was like that in my reign… never surprised at what people did. I think the ordinary people - the farmers and merchants - liked me. *Charlie with the ladies*… and who was it now? They knew I was more interested in that than religion and persecutions, unlike Titus Oates. The minute I laid eyes on him, I knew his sort. People may have thought me a fool, but I kept my head and crown, so I can't have been can I?

It's a pity what happened afterwards, with my brother James. He could have kept the crown and throne if he had been sensible. His daughters were greedy, and I never liked them, or imagined where they would end up... still, the pull of the throne is a powerful one, and for some it's worth the risk.

I learnt a lot in the French court, with regard to intrigue and such like... never mind the promiscuity, which fuelled my likes and dislikes. That's how I got to know the currency of pillow talk. More than one in that court told stories which landed them in trouble, and I wasn't going to give the game away to any lady who took my fancy, when I returned to England.

I knew I would return. I felt it with every fibre of my being, but I had to be careful, when discussions opened up. I had no longing for ultimate power, so was open to suggestions, as long as the crown and throne were at my feet. Pity I had no royal son to hand it over to... a great shame! I would have liked to see the Stuart line continue. Instead, you eventually had the bickering Hanoverians. Mind, I get on very well with George the Third. He is a very gracious man indeed, and not the mad king he is proposed to be.

That's all I have to say... some things are best left unsaid... and you probably wouldn't be interested in the intrigues of my court, as they revolved mainly around my room.

Charles

RAPHAEL

I AM NO FOOL
(07/12/17 - 15:45)

Sometimes I am taken for a soft and gentle soul, because of the velvet undertones to my heart and soul. It is when a nefarious individual - of whom I have a lot in my charge and care - think they can pull the wool over my eyes, then realised they cannot do anything of the sort. I have the advantage you see. I always will have, because it can be no other.

…But, I am being rude, and you may be wondering who this Raphael is? *Skylark* may know who I am, because I have communicated with her before… but not any of you. I hope I do not have to in person. I say this because I am a highly-developed soul, of messianic experience and understanding. It is my role in heaven, to keep under my watchful eye, all the people who have enacted deeds of a despicable nature. So, I cannot be any other than a wise and learned soul. There is one thing I have which they do not, and that is love within every atom of my being. I bring love with me when I have to counsel or reprimand. I say reprimand, as I am often told to 'go away' in unsavoury language. I sometimes ignore it and continue anyway… and on others, give a firm reply and then carry on. I need to be strong, because each soul under my care has to turn their face to the light… so, I cannot give up on them, no matter what.

I am responsible for a lot of well-known individuals at the moment, along with a vast amount of people who think they have slipped through Earth's justice. Well, let me tell you, this is possible and often happens, but when it is time to pass to spirit, the karmic bill is levied and has to be met, if it does not begin beforehand. So, for any of you thinking you can get away with it; you cannot, because the scales of karma need to be balanced, well and truly. You will linger in solitary conditions for as long as it takes. I care, of course I do, but this Earth cannot continue as it is, so you all need to understand in the plainest of language, that what you do reflects in your heart and soul, and the bill has to be paid.

There, now that is in the open I can continue with other things, and tell you a little about me and some of my co-workers. I am vastly experienced, and I don't need to explain why, as I think you can guess the need for it. I am not the only one, as I have hundreds to help me, and each one has the light of God in their heart. They need to have, as I will not tolerate cruelty towards any soul. I am good friends with Jesus and the prophet Moses, and both will step in and help, if the need is there. I have had to ask, as it goes, because during the crusades, knights were killed in battle and they needed a stern hand on arrival. Jesus spoke to a lot of them, saying in no uncertain terms *'Not in my name... I do not expect such behaviour from any who claim to be Christian!'*

One of the kings, from the kingdom of Great Britain, proved to be a highly expletive soul, but he behaves himself now, and is proving to be adept at channeling the healing energy to his old country... and he doesn't roar like a lion any more.

Moses spoke to the high priest Caiaphas, and told him plainly that his behaviour was unfitting for a man claiming to be Jewish. He also helped out with a few other high priests and kings of Judah, who were not mindful of the people they were supposed to have cared for (Solomon and Rehoboam to name but two).

You will hear a little later on from Jonah, who has helped a great many turn their face to the light and walk a different path. I admire him for the grace and generosity he has always shown, even when being shouted at by a rude and ignorant person, he was trying to help. Jonah will never back down and neither will I.

What else can I tell you? I also have some lovely angelic-like souls who are female, as sometimes a gentle female presence can calm the mind. Susanna is one of them, and at the moment she is trying to help a Roman emperor, who still thinks he is a god... Caligula is his name... Titus is another, but that's a different story and situation, as Moses had a few words with him too. If you think about it, Caligula died a long time ago, yet is still raving like he did when he was emperor. He chooses to... simple as that!

What he doesn't realise is that Susanna knows he is putting on an act, on the occasions when he is trying to look 'saintly.' She can tell that the minute her back is turned, he would be yelling for her execution… and that we cannot allow. So, he continues whining and blaming everybody but himself for his plight. He will remain for as long as it takes, until he shows true humility and the beginning of love in his heart. If we were to let him mingle in the lower levels, then 'like attracts like,' so all have to be separated. It means the ego isn't fed, or plans made which cannot be allowed to grow… and, we can easily prevent them if they did.

I would like to stress that we are never cruel or intolerant, but if you are a terrorist or a trafficker of children or adults, you are never allowed to continue peddling in what makes you feel powerful. You only have to look at the plight of some young women in the world, to know that they are taken advantage of and sold into prostitution, to be abused and mistreated cruelly. A lot of these men have families, so how do you think they would feel if the tables were reversed? Gives food for thought, doesn't it. Often the wives are complicit in their partner's activities, and share in the profits of misery. They are not forgotten in the karmic consequences. I am disgusted, but I can never show it because it would mean I have dropped to their level… I am too bright and evolved for that.

I think I have said enough for the moment, but I will be back in later writings, to explain further one or two things. Until then may the face of God shine upon you, and bring hope to your hearts.

*****

HATSHEPSUT

A PHARAOH WITH A NEW NAME
(09/12/17 - 11:37)

I am no longer known by my name of Hatshepsut. I was a woman with a purpose, in an ambitious, man's world. I could be as cruel as cruel could be. I felt I had to make people fear me… and I did! I also had a chosen man who was my lover. He was discreet, as he knew he had to be; otherwise I would have poisoned him. Yet I - the woman with unlimited power - was curtailed by a man called Raphael, and I hated him for it to begin with. He is now my friend, and I am much happier, as I do not have to behave as a man any more, or look like one, which wasn't difficult in the land of my ancestors.

At the very start of my journey - after I had died - I did not know where I was. I thought I had been kidnapped, yet the pain I felt in my mind and body was no longer with me; so I rejoiced and shouted for wine. None appeared though. No one came to do my bidding, so I shouted even louder and cursed like no female should. I stalked like a lion ready to kill, and felt like it too. Where were my slaves and my female attendants? Where was my court of scheming sycophants, ready to do my bidding and kill at my word? I shouted more but still none came, and I could not leave the confines of where I was. It felt like an eternity before a man approached me. He did not bow or grovel in my presence. 'How dare you not bow on your knees, you worm of a man' I roared. He looked at me with love in his eyes, and I was momentarily silenced. I looked back at him, and he looked and never flinched, or lowered his gaze. I screamed even louder, with curses that shook my soul… but not his. Still he said nothing and then, when I was silent, simply said 'have you finished, or do you wish to say more?'

I knew he was high born, from the manner in which he spoke to me. His words cut me like none before, yet he was graceful as he spoke. I asked him who he was and he said that he was Raphael; keeper of the souls of the damned. I said no, I was mightier than he, and I had never heard his name before. He told me that my power was fleeting; it had no currency here, and he left.

I did not see him for a long time after that. I felt lonely, hungry and thirsty, and I shouted for him to bring me grapes, watermelons and wine… still I was ignored. Then I had nightmares, which I will not speak about, but it was like they were with me night and day; tormenting me as though I had done wrong. How could I as pharaoh ever do wrong in the eyes of the gods? My torments were of my own doing and making, and I see that now, as I am no longer the woman I was. I have Raphael to thank for that. He was and is the kindest and gentlest of souls, and I am proud to say that he considers me a friend. It took a lot for me to understand that the gods were not gods, but the creation of the minds of men, and that as pharaoh, I had been unjust and cruel. I accept this now, but it was not easy at the start of my journey, with him.

I am no longer Hatshepsut, so I look at my people of Egypt with a new vision. I see men and women with light in their eyes, and not servants to do my bidding. I have been shown how to channel energy to them, and I do so with joy. I may no longer consider myself a mighty pharaoh, but I still have a place in my heart for the men and women from the land of my ancestors, and always will have.

I have lived other lives since, and learnt a lot from my guides, which means I am making progress, otherwise I would not be allowed to tell a little of my story to you. Matthias is of course here, keeping his eye on my letter, but I know that *Skylark* would question any wrong on my behalf. Yet, I am not who I was, and would not be allowed to reincarnate if I were. I am experiencing new things all the time, in the lives I am offered.

Sometimes I think to myself, that I am so fortunate to have met Raphael, as without his help and guidance and that of my guides, I would not be the woman I am becoming. I thank them so much for their generosity of heart and soul.

With blessings to you all.

AUGUSTUS (formally known as)

MY STATUS MATTERS NO MORE
(09/12/17 - 15:40)

What I do now is more important to me than whom or what I was. The contacts I like to have are different to what I wanted in my reign, as leader of the Roman world, and eventually a god to boot... on the subject of boot... 'Little Boots' is an abomination, and I was disgusted at what Claudius told me about his time as emperor. I have to say that a few of us from my family were odd and peculiar. I always thought that Claudius was top of that list and an utter fool. I was the fool - not him - and blind to a lot of things. My ambition clouded me in many ways. I wanted more than revenge for the murder of Julius (Caesar), by the high and mighty of Rome. I wanted top of that dung heap, and got it with war and death on my way up. I was rewarded with nitwits in the family, along with a legacy to be ashamed of.

I never liked Tiberius... my wife Livia's son. Always thought him a bit 'iffy,' it turns out I wasn't wrong. You know, he still lingers with perverse thoughts ever running through his mind. He will recover, as worse than him have.

So, how did I get to this stage, where I am allowed to communicate a letter to you all? One name says it all... Raphael... the most glorious of souls... a true messianic figure, and healer of the less than enlightened souls, in the lower levels of heaven. He helped me a lot and didn't tolerate my rudeness, or threatening to have him executed on the spot, for disobeying me. I was rude as rude can be, and didn't know where I was when I died. I barked my orders left, right, and centre, and bellowed like a bull when I spoke. I was still emperor in my mind, and a formidable soldier.

When I was in battle, I never wavered or showed fear. I gloried in the defeat of my enemies, especially if they were of the senate and chivalrous (if any of them were). So, I quite enjoyed my climb to the top... more than I dare admit. I might even have taken Julius on, if the conditions were right... who knows?

97

So, what got me here? As time went by, Raphael asked a family member who was well on the way to becoming a little more enlightened, to talk to me. He asked this particular man because he thought it would shock some sense into me, and hopefully bring about the realisation of where I was. Yes, it did on both accounts. Dare I say it but it was Claudius.

He came this day, and greeted me as though we were brothers. I looked at him and asked what he thought he was doing, and was told that I was no longer emperor. 'Who is?' I roared. 'A man called Domitian' came the reply. 'What! Who's that... never heard of him?'
'No, you won't have' said Claudius, 'because you are dead!'
There plain and simple. I couldn't take it from Raphael, but if Claudius said it, then that was different. He had no ambition, no axe to grind against me, and I thought Raphael had. When he told me that he had eventually been emperor, I said 'You - a fool - as emperor... I must be dead for that to happen!' Of course, I would have been with the gods, if he sat where I had.

I wanted to know everything that went on after me? He told me what he knew, and alluded to what he thought may have happened. What a family! At least Tiberius was adopted, and not directly related to me... unlike Caligula and Nero.

I have moved on a lot, thanks to Raphael. I am prepared to explore my karma in the lives I have been offered, and I am learning... always learning. I am not the man I was, as Augustus, so I no longer use that name. I have had many names since then, but one in particular I like, and that is 'John.' I also use it out of respect for an angelic-like figure, who works so hard for nature. That is the John who Rose briefly mentioned... a man with such an astonishing depth of knowledge, and unlimited patience. When he sees's waste dumped or the sea further polluted with plastic products, he is never angry; because he knows it will change, and the Earth will one day be treated with greater respect.

I admire him a lot, and try to help as much as I can, in my small way. *It is the small ways that count,* he once told me, because if we all did one tiny thing to benefit nature, it would help the world more than we realise.

*****

CLAUDIUS

I NEVER WANTED IT
(10/12/17 - 11:43)

It's true; I never wanted to be emperor, as I had witnessed too much to wish to sit where my family had. They stank of ambition and none more so than Tiberius, with the help of his scheming mother. You may think this is all fanciful, and it cannot be proven, but feel the energy of the written word and that will help.

I loved my wife Messalina a great deal, and was blind to her wants and demands. It was cruel to the children to have her executed, but that's what happened… I can't change history and neither can you. If it was possible, then I would have liked to prevent Caligula becoming emperor, and the outbreak of world war one, because then it just might be a different world. I know that *Skylark* feels the same about one of my choices, but nothing can be done… or can it?

Can we prevent despots, atrocities and war? If the will is there maybe, but to interfere in other countries, like the varying empires of this world is another story. I liked my empire as Claudius, but not as who I am now. My guide Robert said to me, that I never really had a chance to be any other than who I was, as Claudius. I was murdered, so we can put that straight here and now, and stop speculation. I knew it would occur, as my last wife was my niece Agrippina, and she reminded me of her brother Caligula, so it was bound to happen. I saw it in her eyes… they were so like his, as though they were dead to life. That's how he looked sometimes. His eyes showed no emotion, much like a shark's as it is prowling, looking to feed… and Caligula fed on the blood of the senate.

Mind you, a lot of the powerful men and women did that. Sometimes the women of Rome were as ambitious as their husbands. You only need to consider Augustus' wife, Livia, for that. Oh, I could tell you stories about her, that would make Robert Graves' books about me and my family seem like bedtime stories. I quite like them as it goes, and the BBC series which is a favourite of *Skylark's,* from when she was a young woman. That's why the actor, John Hurt, at her request, will communicate a letter in a later book, because of a particular scene. He played Caligula and Derek Jacobi was cast as me. I would like to thank Derek a lot, as I was thrilled at what he did. Many of us were on set watching. It was exciting; there is no doubt about that. All of the actors were marvellous, and I wish to say thank you... but for me, it is a special heartfelt thank you to Derek.

I lingered like Augustus did, but I was open to the words spoken to me, so I looked at the light and stepped into it. That is why Raphael asked me, and no other, to talk to Augustus, as he never hid from me that he thought I was an imbecile. I didn't mind one bit, as I thought him a bully and was glad to be kept out of the limelight. I was glad to be of service though, and help him if I could. We are on good terms now; he is a much different man and so am I.

It is actually my guide Robert communicating this letter, as I have reincarnated. I managed to write with *Skylark* to explain beforehand, so she knows that I recorded what I wished to say. It's all in the Akashic Records, clear as clear can be, so Robert can't go wrong. My current life will evolve, I hope, where I shall explore the metaphysical. I will be no medium, but I might put my toe in the water, so in my next life, it builds up and I want to learn more.

Mediumship isn't for everybody, but it is within the soul, so at the correct stage of development the interest opens up... it's the same as for absent healing. We can all learn how to do it, but if the television and the material life are more important, so be it. As the lives build up, and a person has lived over thirty, then the spiritual becomes a wider door through which to walk. I have learnt a lot from Isaiah Abbotsbury's open circle. Quite a few of us have, as he is a skilled soul. He taught *Skylark* everything she knows, and look at her writing with a man once thought to be an idiot... and an ex-emperor to boot!

On the subject of emperors - you won't have any more in this book, but in later ones. Royalty is a different story. One or two are lining up with excitement, ready to go at a moment's notice, and a gentle soul called David is one of them.

I think I have said enough. I would like to go on a bit more and tell you about Livia, but she was rather an unsavoury character, so best not!

With the greatest of respect,
Claudius

GOD

I AM JUST A MAN WITH A POINT OF VIEW
(12/12/17 - 08:12)

Is that what you think? Or maybe I am a dominant male with a taste for biblical oracles; where I rail against nations who attack my people? I do not like war or injustice, no matter who it is against. Neither do I like social media, but then again, if I was on Facebook could I reach out to more of you? Would I come up against trolls and have vile slanders against me, or just have good and simple death threats? My sons had those. All of the messiahs', men and women, that have walked this Earth had death threats, because of their outspokenness, goodness and generosity. It would have been easier to silence them than give an answer. You see, I like a good debate, and I like to witness charity and goodness of heart and soul; but I do not always get to see it… and now, the spirit of the lord will come upon *Skylark,* and I will prophecy… I haven't done so for quite a while, and I like to enjoy myself from time to time. Peoples of the world hearken, and you can choose to listen or not…

*…I say to you that I am a loving God, and wish only goodness for each and every one of you, so do not destroy this planet you inhabit… because if you continue as you are doing, in **fifty** years' time, it will be a different state of affairs. It will also be different for the major nations of the world, because times will change, so that cars have to be cleaner and more efficient. Of course, there will be new-fangled inventions, to further stretch your pockets, when they do not need to.*

I say against the people that traffic men, women, and children, that you will meet the most enlightened of souls. His name is Raphael, and if you are lucky you will not linger… if you turn your face to the light, as Claudius did, and step into it.

I also say to people that bomb, maim, and kill, that perhaps in a future life, on a different planet, you will experience what you decided to give.

I say to the people of Syria, that I love you so much… do not think that

I AM *is not with you, because I am. Every fibre of my heart and my soul is yours, if you will ask of me... you only have to call and I will answer.*

I say to the people of Iraq, that you are blessed, and although times have been so difficult, it will change, because abominations have to stop, and I do not like it done in my name. ***NEVER KILL IN DEFENCE OF ME, OR USE MY NAME TO JUSTIFY MURDER!*** *Neither do I like courts that give sentences, where I am used to bring misery and fear to heart and soul. I do not like courts which are unjust and pretend to be righteous and godly.*

The puffin is a delightful little bird that I love very much, and will never be extinct, and neither will the octopus.

Do not destroy the waters of the Earth, for they are more valuable than you realise. The deep has secrets which I do not wish for you to explore, because you could destroy the fabric of the life of the sea. It is your choice, and always will be, but do not blame or call on me if you walk a path you cannot change. I will give you fifty years to build upon the knowledge that if the sea fails, so will the balance of the planet.

If no changes are made, then Rose will say loud and clear what needs to be done. It will be your choice to listen, or not, because I will not have you say that you were not warned, or blame Rose for the outcome. She will not be alone, as my blessed friend Judas Iscariot will reincarnate, along with many others, at the same time. You will not tell who is who, so do not try.

I know that the sky is blue, but if you do not clean up the planet it will begin to turn grey.

There will be night visitors one August, many years away. They come with my love and blessing, and will teach you a lot.

I bless each and every one of you and would like to say more. I cannot, as you might think that I am unjust, but justice is not mine to give... karma is completely different, as it is never unjust.

To the people that maim and destroy in the Middle East, remember that you are under my watchful eye. I see everything, and I mean

*EVERYTHING... and I do not like it! I may bless you and still love you, but I cannot say that I like what you do. I bless you my peoples, and remember that it is **I AM**, and not Skylark, who channels these words. Also remember that I love each and every one of you, and so does Raphael, but he will speak to those that need his love and counselling... and so will the people whose lives you affect, as they will want to know 'why.' Sometimes it is not always easy, but so be it, as that is the way of your world, and not mine.*

Amen

LEVI

GOD IS MY FRIEND… HE WAS WITH ME IN BERGEN-BELSEN CONCENTRATION CAMP
(12/12/17 - 08:26)

Good morning to you all. I would like to use the greeting *'shalom'* to my brothers and sisters of Israel.

I died in the concentration camp called Belsen, but I never forgot God while I lived, and he stood with me every moment I spent in that hellish place. He was there as the guards beat me, and I felt his love and witnessed it flow into the men that spat and kicked me. Some of my friends in the camp thought that God had abandoned them. I would say Hashem knew into the heart of man, and the day of judgement would come at the appointed time. *We would rise and be with him because I have seen his glory and I know that it is good.*

I was not always believed, but then I was asked questions about my ideas. *'He has forgotten us,'* I was told more than once. I would say *'no, he has not; his love is evident, even here, if we reach out with our minds.'* Fear held me back on many occasions, when I was desperate to know he was with me. Yet, I firmly believe, even with the fear I felt, that he still touched my heart. Although I never felt joy, I did experience a sort of love, when I looked at the faces of the guards. They looked evil, and I can't say any other, yet I tried to see the light of God in them; as I thought he would be everywhere, and not in the ruins of a once glorious temple, which was part of our heritage.

I now know without a doubt, that each Jew, gypsy, or individual who suffered at the hands of the Third Reich had a guardian angel with them, and never walked the road to heaven alone. They had the Good Samaritan of the parable in the scriptures (*Luke 10:29-37)* who went beyond what was necessary, with no idea other than to give help where it was needed. He transcended human thought. He did not need to think what to do, he did it instinctively… and God is just like that! He does not think… *he does*… and that my friends is the true nature of light, and the light of the world; as it does not need human thought or emotion.

I rejoiced when I arrived in the arms of God. I met my family, and we sang together like we had never done before. I hope that my journey lets you know that we are not abandoned, no matter where the road takes us.

With blessings to you all, and know this... I am alive and not waiting for the day of salvation, because for me it is already here.

Amen

(As Levi draws near and shows himself, he is an orthodox Jew, a religious man and a teacher - *Skylark*).

JONAH

AS THE LIGHT SHINES, THE VEIL IS LIFTED
(13/12/17 - 08:53)

Not everybody can see the light at first, because they are blind to it; through the darkness of their personal outlook. Adolf Hitler is like this and so is Josef Stalin. They are both blind to the light of God. Mr. Hitler is whining and blaming everybody but himself, much like Caligula is.

I am strong, so I cannot be fooled. I see the aura and hear the thoughts in the lower vibration of the aura, so there is no use in trying to pull the wool over my eyes, as I would see straight through it. We do not read minds - none of us can - but if the thought is strong enough, it will permeate the baser levels of the person's aura, and the more skilled spirit plane soul can easily sense and read what is there.

Perhaps I had better give a formal introduction. My name is Jonah, and I am one of the highly-skilled souls who help Raphael. I am actually one of his deputies; not through hierarchy, but skill and experience. I have been in this area of work for some time, so I have seen it all. Nothing surprises me. I am glad that it doesn't, because then I am not shaken or stirred by the expletives or obscene gestures which are often flung my way... once a bully always a bully... unless you come under the care of Raphael and his co-workers. Nothing stops us, no matter how long it takes... and it is never a threat to be with us, because we are determined that all faces will turn to the light, and face the truth of their lives.

How to do it if you are in the lower levels of spirit? Well, at first you are left to calm down, as quite often people are fiery and in the thick of it; especially if it is a battle like the knights of old fought. Then one of us will go to have a little chat and introduce ourselves. After that, follows the usual insults, and attempts at bribery and corruption... except for Claudius, the Emperor of Rome. He stepped into the light quickly, because inside his soul that is what he always wanted, but was led in other directions. There was still an element of time, but for him it was quicker than for a lot.

There will also be a queue lining up, of people who want to ask why you did what you did to them. We do not stop this process, as it is part of karma... but be warned, it can be tricky to experience. Still, if you gave it, then you need to take it! All the while though, you will be sent absent healing to help you cope with the process, and we keep an eye out, to constantly see what is going on. Caligula and Adolf Hitler find it a living nightmare, but that is what they gave to others, so they must experience the consequences of it.

Perhaps some of this may frighten you, but don't worry it is only for the nefarious individuals who peddle in atrocities, that come under our wing. If you are not a drug dealer or terrorist, people trafficker or other such individual, who brings injury or death through malicious intent, then you are okay. You may have people wanting to ask you questions, if you were President of the United States of America, during the gulf war, for example. That is natural, as I would want to understand, and *Skylark* gets this. She finds that if she can understand something, it helps her to deal with it, so it's perfectly normal that people will want to say 'hey what was such and such all about?'

So, what's the next step in the process? Talk to your guide and face what you have done... that will help as he/she will have seen everything. It will also be on record in the Akashic Records, so no fooling your guide. If it's me that you are with, then I take it step by step, and can see if you are trying to trick me. All the time I am allowing my aura to slowly shine brighter and brighter, as that is healing in itself, and accustoms the person to brighter conditions. Once I see and feel that the time is right, then I channel a lot of healing energy to your aura. It can be painful for a brief moment, as it was for Simon de Montford for example, but then love flows into the soul and the process of rehabilitation can begin, on the first level of the spirit plane, in the Halls of Rest. The rehabilitation process is for another day and book, but in a nutshell that is a pared down edition of what happens.

I would expect when some of you read this, you may feel WHOOOOAH, don't like the sound of that! Well if you don't, then don't do the things that require it in the first place! For some people karma means that the process can begin in their current life, with unpleasant events occurring, if the balance needs to begin earlier, through what has been done. It is no surprise Adolf Hitler took his own life, because he knew he would be in for a tough time and tried to avoid it... but hasn't! But, and take note, listen to this... you can also see life differently, seek help, and start something good in your life, which will begin to balance your karma. Being an okay and helpful person is not woosy or weak and feeble, because it takes strength to take a long good look at yourself and walk another path.

Don't throw acid is a good place to start at. A dreadful thing to do! Yep, do much of that, and I shall look you in the eye, and it won't affect me one bit any shenanigans you try.

Know also, that we never blame anybody in spirit, because quite often the person does that for themselves... so don't expect finger wagging from us. We never do it and neither does God or Gabriel. I say 'Gabriel', as there is the idea that he has trumpets and the dead shall arise. 'No' to that, but I hope by now you will already have worked that one out.

I am a strong and evolved soul and I love and respect all in my care, but if I back down, then love will take longer to flow into the heart and soul. What I do, I do out of love and for love.

With blessings to you all,
Jonah

A ROMAN LIBRARIAN

I KNOW IT ALL, SO FAR
(15/12/17 - 15:06)

I have known the story of everything written so far, regarding the movement which became known as Christianity. I have also seen what is lying ahead to be transcribed. More will come, that will explain to the current keepers of the secret documents, so they can see the bigger picture. Just as Flavius is scarred, so is Marcus, and quite badly on his face. That has been written down and can be checked for accuracy if desired. His scar runs down the left side of his face, and has left its impact, so he shows little emotion due to the nerves affected. It happened during one savage battle, and Flavius saved his life, otherwise who knows what would have happened. Could God have stepped in and saved him? 'I don't know' is the answer to that, but it has happened to more than one soldier in Afghanistan, that had a lucky escape.

I am nobody in the grand schemes of things… nothing special at all! I was a simple man who knew how to keep a secret, and who had an interest in books; until I was chosen to be one of the keepers of the documents of the early church. I have seen every single item which has been recorded, and I am appalled that no-one, so far, has spoken out. I knew that if I had done, at the time, then I could have been in a lot of trouble... maybe even my life would have been in danger. So, I kept silent and felt I could do nothing else. I am now sorry that I did; I wish I had braved the furore, and said what I felt I needed to. Now I can because I cannot be harmed, as I am already in heaven.

*****

LEO

I KEPT SILENT
(15/12/17 - 15:22)

I had a taste for the fineries in life, and I liked wine, women, and song… not in that particular order, but I enjoyed all three, and more than one courtesan was paid for their silence. That was nothing unusual for some of the many popes (and Leos), who sat in the seat of power, as head of the one true church. But is it? Is it as true as people think? Back then I would say 'no' - but now - now is different, as I think Francis is a wonderful man… so unlike me. I am pleased for that, as the church needs an honourable person as its head.

I too have seen everything - up to the point of my death - which had been collected on the foundation of the early church. It is a lot different to what the scriptures show it to be. Women were included and encouraged to be vocal, as Phoebe, an early apostle, was an important woman who prophesied with great accuracy. I saw what she said. Not everything, as I doubt the church has it all, but some of the words she channeled are very accurate to this day. There were no speaking in tongues back then, as it was said in the local language, so everyone could understand… much more sensible, and less of a waste of time, if nobody could translate the word of the Holy Spirit.

I was a greedy pope… a lot of us were like that, and hungry for power. If what I know had been made common knowledge, it could have saved many lives and perhaps prevented a lot of wars. I am sorry and should have done something, but I didn't as I wanted no woman to challenge me. Warm my bed, yes, and satisfy my needs, but nothing else. I didn't like women in power… rich women, yes, as they could be used for political motives… so, I could see how they could be useful… but for no other reason.

So, why should I have spoken out? I probably wouldn't have been believed at the time, and maybe even silenced, myself. It is never too late to tell the truth. I understand that now, and have followed my karmic path accordingly. The steps to salvation, on my road, have not been the simplest, but then what do I expect… a pat on the back?

*****

GOD

THE TRUTH WILL ALWAYS BE MADE AVAILABLE, TO THOSE WHO ASK
(15/12/17 - 15:53)

I always speak the truth, and so do my sons and daughters in spirit. None lie, unless they are on the lower levels, and then they will eventually speak the truth, on their healing journey. It is difficult to lie, as you need to keep check on who has been told what. For those of you who do, you must know that it's not always simple, or easy, to follow the path of your words. I can see in the aura if an untruth has been told, or an exaggeration and such like. Your guides can too, but what has been kept hidden for so long needs to come out, because it is too important to remain buried any longer.

It will be an interesting journey for everyone involved, including Isaiah and Tilly Abbotsbury, and *Skylark*. Each of them knows something that you don't, but the reality is that it is very little in the scheme of it. *Skylark* knows the most of the three of them, but then she has studied scripture and sat at her kitchen table with her atlas and dictionaries, looking and checking, and wondering what's what. She has read through many books, including ones by C.S.Lewis, and Christian and Jewish scholars. Her guides have written with her and given her information intuitively, but it was she who realised that my son Yeshua had not been crucified. We left it for her to find out the truth, because she had told her guides that she did not want to know from them, because it was 'too big a lie!'

So, *Skylark* needed to sort the wheat from the chaff herself... and she did! Can you do the same? I do not blame any of you if you feel angry, but know this... that I am real! I am not a fabrication or an illusion, yet I am not who the scriptures portray me to be. Jesus, Mary and Joseph were real people, but not called by those names. Did you know that Mary and Joseph had a disabled son, called Simon? You will soon, because Simon will tell you a little about his life, on the pages which lie ahead.

Ask me what you will, and I shall try to answer in the most

appropriate ways I can. For now though, read on and face the future with hope because you will, over the remaining years of *Skylark's* life, meet some of the hardest workers for mankind, who gave of their heart and soul.

*****

JOSEPH

MY SON
(18/12/17 - 10:06)

My name, to the world, is thought to be Joseph, and some even think me an old man when I married. Yet, I was far from elderly when I died in an accident. My eldest boy was still young, but he spoke eloquently at my funeral, and all of my family sent their love to me on the wings of a dove. So, what is my name if it is not Joseph, and how did I become a man unknown, yet important to the story?

My name is **Josiah,** so it is not that far from the truth. Translators did not quite understand the lingua franca of my home town, but that is not important in the scheme of things. Yet it is and very much so, because if my name was misunderstood then, so could a lot have been… and it was! It is easy for me to say this because you cannot argue with me, as I am unable to answer unless it is through the hand of a little bird. I will come again to tell you more and more of my life, and my love for my family. For now though, remember that the word of God is always one of truth, and his prophecy echoes down the millennia.

Leo spoke about an apostle and prophetess called Phoebe, in his recent letter. She prophesied with eloquence, and these can still be read on scraps of parchment, locked away yet not gathering dust. They will see the light of day again, and be checked for accuracy, against what others say on the page of this and future books. I am barely mentioned, but then again would I be if my bones had desiccated and turned into the dust of the ground. Yet my sons are… and Simon was not forgotten by God, when Phoebe spoke. A boy when he died, whose voice will ring clear again, once his mother has spoken. I was not an old man when I died and my family grieved for me, but they knew without a doubt that I was close to them, on the journey they made to the land of the pharaohs.

*****

MARY

OUR JOURNEY WAS DIFFERENT
(18/12/17 - 10:35)

My husband has just spoken to you and now it is my turn. I cannot and will not say everything which needs to be translated, but I can make a start. To begin with my name is not Mary, but **Ruth.** How I became Mary is a story in itself, with a bit of misunderstanding of my name thrown in. Not everyone was skilled at translating the oral tradition of story-telling, and many states and tribes had different ways of pronunciation. It is not that bad, compared to other things. I do need to put one or two things straight, and one of them is that Jesus had brothers and sisters, who were of his blood. Josiah and I had many children, as we were married young... Jesus was not the oldest, and Simon not the youngest. We were a happy family, and Jesus never ignored us or spoke against us once. How could a man as he do anything of such a nature? We were an important part of his life and ministry. His love was so generous that he could give of himself to any and all... and he did!

Simon was the most intelligent of all my children, who lived beyond the first few days of life. He was so bright and generous that you could do nothing other than love him. His disabilities meant nothing to me, because I saw through them, to the love in his soul. When I gave birth to him, women told me to put him out for the hyenas, *'to do what you cannot.'* I said 'no,' he was my child and I loved him, and that was it. He was loved by all the family. God stood with him, and I could see that for myself.

We often were aware of God with us, as sometimes we felt a gentle breeze which soothed us. We knew then who it was that brought the wind of love, to cool us down as we walked. On other occasions, we found water where we did not expect to, and a man with a willing hand to help us dig for it. God looked after us wherever we were. He stood with Simon when he died, ready to lift him into his arms, and take him to the bosom of Abraham.

I did not weep because I knew Simon would never leave me. He needed a little time to know where he was... that was it! I felt the stroke of his hand on my hair one night, and knew it was him bringing his love to me in the way only he knew how. I was never afraid to die, but I did not want to see Jesus nailed to a stake and mocked. I would have done anything to stop that. I did not have to, as Marcus and Flavius prevented a cruel and unjust death. They were not alone, as Jesus was loved by a great many soldiers, who were ready to help him, just as he helped them. I thank them for it, because without their solidarity a lot of things could have been different.

*****

SIMON

JUDAS ISCARIOT WAS THE BEST FRIEND
A BOY COULD HAVE
(18/12/17 - 11:18)

I am Simon, the son of Josiah and Ruth. They were the kindest and most loving parents to me. My friend, Judas Iscariot, was also kind and loving. Judas has been wronged over the years for betraying my brother Yeshua, but he did not and never would have, because he loved him just as much as me… the word 'Judas' is still used to refer to acts of betrayal, and I can no longer stay silent about it.

Judas was my best friend when I was on the Earth. We are close now, and think of each other as brothers. It hasn't been easy for him or the Jewish people, of whom I am one, to be associated with the death of a messiah. *Skylark* had it said to her once that the Jews killed Jesus, and she knows they did not. She is also on good terms with Judas and thinks of him as the brightest of the bright. He has helped her with absent healing and was present at some of her bible study group meetings… of which she was aware. He has also told her a little about his family and home life, and about how we met. My mother Ruth has also spoken to *Skylark* about that. Not in any great depth, but enough to know that he was respected by my family, and how he missed me very much when I was no longer with him in the physical body.

It has been terrible to think how he has been blamed for an injustice, which never occurred. The years of insults and liturgies which have involved his name have to stop. Now is that time, to clear away the debris of history, and say once and for all, that *my friend did not in any way betray my family or my brother!*

*****

MAY (MARY OF TECK)

I LOVE MY COUNTRY VERY MUCH
(18/12/17 - 12:03)

When I was queen, I was very aware of my responsibilities. One of the worst acts of betrayal, to my mind, was that of my son Edward. He is called David by his family, but some of you may not realise that, if you do not live in Great Britain. I shall refer to him as David, if you do not mind.

I felt that we, as a family, had privileges beyond what others had. We were loved - I thought - by the people, even during difficult times. My husband, the king, did not agree with me, and was concerned that we would be overthrown, like Russian royalty. I did not think so, but I was a woman and my voice had never been accurately heard; unlike that of your present queen.

It hasn't been easy for Elizabeth, as the royal family has had to move with the times, and be more open. People think we are paid well for the work we undertake. I have to agree, but think on this… that what we do is often scrutinized down to the smallest detail, and sometimes we can do no right. Now that I have that off my chest, I can continue.

David was my son and I loved him, but I didn't like his lifestyle. The comments he made about people, and some of the friends he chose were beyond the pale. He did not take his responsibility seriously, and I think he was afraid of it. His father did not help, as he often berated him in front of the family, and did not understand his human frailty. As a family, we did not always 'gel,' which wasn't helped by the expected protocol. I would sometimes think that if it had all been different, would David have been the man fit to be king? I do not know if I am honest, but I love him nonetheless.

*****

DAVID WINDSOR

I AM JUST A MAN
(18/12/17 - 12:37)

My experiences in world war one shook me to the core, and I never felt the same after. It was nothing compared to what other men had to deal with, as I couldn't be openly placed in the line of fire. Still, it affected me more than anyone ever realised. I never even spoke to Wallis about it… and that is saying something.

I was never the man to be king, and should not have had that responsibility placed on my shoulders. They were not broad enough to cope, and I couldn't have done it without the woman whose strength I absorbed. Sometimes I wonder if my choice of wife was an act of rebellion, against the stifling environment of royal life. Either way it was not a happy marriage.

Once Wallis was away from the family, and knew she would not have all the titles she thought due to her, it was a different thing. I most certainly regretted it, as she had little love inside her soul, and certainly not for me in private. I began to despise her, and felt a little frightened too, as the years went on. I even wondered if I had made a mistake. I felt homesick for the dreariness of the British winter and the local lingua franca. I could say little - if anything - apart from in my notebooks. At least, to write some of it down gave me a small feeling of relief.

I watched from afar, and always took an interest in what my brother and his family did. I am sorry that I placed that burden on him, and have told him so. At the time I wasn't, as I didn't feel up to the role of king, and wanted to avoid it if I could. Maybe Wallis was the perfect excuse?

*****

MICHAEL

SECRETS AND LIES
(27/02/18 - 15:32)

My working life was full of it... misinformation, spin, the lot... and I revelled in getting to the truth of it all. Of course I gave back what I was given, but I liked to think I was good at what I did... and hardly anybody ever got the better of me, as I always took it as a little bit of a personal challenge. I paid prostitutes for a good night's work, and doormen to verify who came and left at what time... and importantly, who they left with. I blackmailed quite a few for the good of queen and country, and I am not ashamed to say so. What I am ashamed of is that I did it, but I am still a patriot; I do the best for my country from spirit side, and I hope for the world. This means that I still look, listen and try to find out what's what, but for very different reasons.

I take an old buddy called John with me. He has recently communicated to *Skylark,* a bit of an excitable letter, of his view on the state of politics in the United Kingdom. Poor chap got quite wound up, so much so that *Skylark* thought she might have to close the letter down and shut off the link. That's what managing your link is all about... stop it if it feels inappropriate! He wasn't being so, or didn't intend to be, but he was - and is - a blunt man, and his vision of our country wasn't going to his plan, so he was a little blunt in his views. He stopped and apologised, and the letter continued and finished; perhaps a little shorter than he intended, but he knows if it is allowed, he can continue with one or two things.

Which brings me onto Janus - yes Janus - and those of you who know will understand what I mean by that. The god, who looks more than one way in mythology, so can turn a blind eye to what he doesn't wish to see... or even be two-faced. Let's go along the route that everything is seen and known about, but that the face given to the world is a different one in private. You know that - those who lurk in the world I inhabited - but do you know that it's worse than you have so far found out? A spider's web is small by comparison, and their web is far bigger than their enemy's; which is considered to be substantial. Janus is rotten though, and could crumble and topple into another's web, but will it be a friendly one? One which will listen intently and be open to persuasion, yet not be easily manipulated? It depends on the insects it catches and plays with, and that depends on the approach of other insects, intent on catching and playing with it.

I am a patriot and always will be, but I am no fool, and will never say anything unless it is for the good of the world. So, work this out my friends of the shade; you will have to work not to be seen by day, and the ploys of old will need to be sparklier and more lustrous. Janus is no fool and neither am I.

Michael

TOMMY COOPER

I LIKED MY ACT WITH THE FEZ
(28/02/18 - 13:43)

I used to make *Skylark* and her family laugh… I am proud of that, and of making many other people laugh. Yet, I never felt like it inside of me.

Would you believe it, if I said that *Skylark*, in her early twenties, used to go to the same pub as me? She thought I looked miserable, and I felt it. I saw her looking at me once and completely ignored her… I was that kind of man! I felt as miserable as miserable could be, and I am now sorry for it.

I don't work with any mediums, despite the odd one thinking I do. Well its official, *I don't*… as it's not my privilege to, or in my karma. If I did, do you think I would bring the upliftment needed? I might do now, but not to the level that a guide would.

People get enthusiastic about guides and a bit confused. When I met mine, after I died, I was well and truly scuppered, as I couldn't get away with anything. Still, he is a great guy, and his name is Samuel. I like him, and I am growing to love him like a brother.

I worked hard at my chosen career, and loved the applause, but I wasn't an easy man. Some of you may know that… and I am sorry for how I treated my wife! She has forgiven me, and I don't deserve it, but we get along well and I am grateful for everything she has done for me.

As you may guess from the title, I liked my fez. I mean no disrespect when I say that, but I felt comfortable in it, and it gave me the chance to hide my true self… and that's why I wore costumes. The Nazi uniform seems tasteless, and I am sorry now, but it was fresh in the minds of a lot of people. I felt I was taking a dig at what, I thought, was a terrible experience for the country, and the world to have gone through. Laughing is good medicine, as long as you do it for the right reasons.

I was bullied at school, so I don't like bullying. I feel sorry for the children and the internet, as it looks like there is no let-up. Well, if I can say one thing, which is my opinion only, is that the people who say nasty words online are hiding their true nature behind a screen. They have a lot of problems, and that's why they do it.

I realised that the kids who bullied me were troubled at home, and that's why they did it. It doesn't always make things better, when you are at the receiving end of it. A bit like trolls and people who hide behind the anonymous nastiness they give. Boy, will they have their work cut out for them, when at the right stage of their life, they meet their maker. You can't get away with anything, no matter what.

It's the same all over the world, no matter where you get to meet your guide and face your karma, so it's best to start looking at it now, if you are peddling in nastiness and trolling people. I don't like it, as you may now see. It's not my life, and I hope when I reincarnate again that I never troll another individual, and I have asked as part of my karma, to never do so.

Who would have thought that a miserable old git like me could get on his soap box... *Skylark* didn't, I can tell you! It's my letter though, and I can say what I will, within the bounds of decency, because if I don't, I won't get another opportunity.

I am a changed man, and I am learning a lot about the universal energy and positive affirmations. *Skylark* is saying 'one' and getting a bit impatient, but it will come and soon for her. She is human you see, and although she may have an understanding of a few things, her physical endurances are a bit tricky... and she wants it done, hence the affirmation and impatience at the result. *Skylark* asked for it as part of her karma, and she knows it, and the end result... so, hang on in there girl... the times they are a changing!

With best wishes to you all,
Tommy
(*...and, I always tell it like it is!*)

124

MARGERY ALLINGHAM

I SAW SPIRIT
(01/03/18 - 16:48)

Hello… my name is Margery, but my friends call me Marge. I died of cancer a few years back, and I felt love at the end, despite the pain. I also saw my nana waiting for me by my bed, and she said to me, *'Marge my girl, it's not long now… but don't worry, I will be there to give you the biggest of hugs.'* I want to say to all of you, don't worry because if it was alright for me, then it will be for you too.

I think it's important to know that, because I was frightened of dying and I needn't have been. We all have to go that way sometime, so none of you need give it a second thought; because the people that help Christopher are loving and kind, and go the extra mile to make sure all is okay. You just ask *Skylark,* because she can tell you something about her mum that you might not believe… I know her mum couldn't at the time…

Simon, the lovely angelic-like soul who guided *Skylark's* mum to the Halls of Rest, was so determined to help, that he did everything he could, before he handed her over to her guide and family. So, if it was like that for us two, then only expect love and kindness from your helper of Christopher's.

I am going to write a new book. I have never stopped writing, and I teach it in spirit. You never know, one of my pupils might end up in print on the Earth one day. *Skylark* won't be the only one to transcribe, and she knows it. It won't happen for a while, because she has got a lot to do before she can retire from her writing.

I would never have stopped; it was only illness that quickened the end of it for me. If I had known what I do now, I think I may have given one or two of mine a bit more of a twist. Never ghosts; as I don't like that kind of thing, despite having attended one or two séances. It's thought that I might have done well… I did, but it wasn't fashionable, and the understanding was different back then.

125

Skylark and I agree on the fact that we don't like ghosts and all that kind of spooky stuff and you will never see her with a Ouija board or advertising séances. It's not her bag, and it never was mine, but I knew what my readers liked, and I would have used my experiences, if called on. I was curious about the 'afterlife' and a little bit afraid, but I never dabbled, because I thought I didn't have the 'gift.' Well, you may be surprised to know that *Skylark* didn't think she had it either, and look at her... she has the whole package... clairaudience, the lot. So, if you are curious, get a good teacher like she did, so you get to learn what's right and wrong, as that's important.

In my next life, I plan to ask for a person to guide and teach me. I want to get it right and help people, because it doesn't have to be about haunted buildings, with a bit of a palaver going on. It's about the spiritual - or metaphysical - and bringing love, support, and guidance to the individual... and not fairground fortune-telling!

You will know, if you ever get to see Isaiah Abbotsbury, then you will get to see what's what. It's my opinion and not to everybody's taste, but that's what I think, and I can say so in my letter. I can say what I like, because I have freewill to do just that. None of us were told by God, or our guides, to 'rein it in.' If anything God had to [rein it in], because he got a bit carried away in the first draft, and *Skylark's* fingers flew like the clappers over the keyboard; surprising even her. Mind, it was a bit of the lovely Judas Iscariot channelling God, so no surprise, as they were both up for it, in the most spiritual of ways.

God is like that - gentle and enthusiastic - never taking; only ever giving... he is also my friend and mentor, and he gives me hope! Jesus does too, because he loves you all so much... he is going to reincarnate again. You won't know it's him, because that's how it has to be, but expect only goodness and love. It will be tough love, but sometimes you have to be strong, in order to bring change for the best, and that's what he will do. You ask the keeper of the records, he knows, as an apostle called Phoebe prophesied it... which means that it was written down for posterity. I shall say no more.

With love to you all,
Marge Allingham

MRS BEETON

NOTHING 'MOCK' ABOUT ME!
(02/03/18 - 16:32)

Enthusiasts of cookery will know what I mean by the title I have chosen, and so does *Skylark,* as she has her mother's copy of one of my books. They used to be all the rage at one time, but now are more or less out of fashion... or unheard of by a few younger people. I don't mind that one bit, because I wrote them out of financial necessity, and I don't have that now.

I did try my best to do what I could to help, as young women were expected to run a home. A lot didn't know how to, and marriage was a surprise to many of them. It wasn't always about love many years ago, when I first married. Connections were important, and if you had some money, then that was even better. Sometimes people felt they were in love when it was infatuation, and the gloss soon came off when the reality of marriage was every day. Is it like this now? Perhaps a little, but not how it was back then. People are still impressed by money and connection and their partner being powerful, but I can tell you with truth, that it doesn't impress Tilly and Isaiah Abbotsbury or *Skylark.* You can name drop all you like, but the connections they have are nothing like the rich and powerful can offer to their partners on the Earth.

I wasn't happy in my marriage and I felt pressure to write my books. There... I have, at last, said it! I love my children very much and I am on good terms with my husband, but we have nothing in common, apart from the love for our family. It's not enough to keep us together, so we go our different ways, with respect for each other. How can we do anything other... as there is no stigma or pressure now to stay in an unhappy marriage.

I have love in abundance, and it's my pathway that energises me and brings me confidence; along with the love and respect of my friends, on level two, in the spirit plane. I am working my way through the levels, which form level two, and learning a lot at the same time. I like to help where I can, and most of all with the children in spirit, who pass over before their parents. I mainly work with the children from India and help Mother Teresa.

I admire her as she gives of her heart and soul, and the love from her inner core shines out and brings joy and hope. Some of the children have been abandoned and others died from starvation, with little love given to them. Yet, there is always hope! We see it so often on the Earth, when kindness is shown to an abandoned child, or one wishing to learn to read and write. We always help the helpers in whatever way we can. We have to be careful though because we cannot interfere. This means that the help is intuitively given, so they have freewill and their own knowledge and experience to guide them. I admire all the people who give so much to abandoned children, wherever it is in the world.

I am not sorry for my life as a writer of books, with recipes and advice in, but look at a lot of cookery books now... they are magnificent! Although *Skylark*, in her own words is a terrible cook, she can still admire a recipe book, with tales to tell and beautiful pictures. So, all you people that meet her might never have cordon bleu cooking, but you will see enthusiasm of a different kind, which is also part of the soul of Isaiah and Tilly Abbotsbury.

With love to you all.

PHOEBE

To channel the words of our creator, God, is to be given a privilege that few are ever given. I spoke words of love from the heart of God, to a beleaguered people often suppressed, and now my voice is given opportunity once again, to sing its song with love for the Earth...

The bear will growl and the ice man will be stalked by it. Yet the man of ice will melt and fall away, as the men of steel rise again to challenge authority.

The voice of a messianic figure will ring out, but not be recognised, and the man of the universe will stand by - yet not idle - in the ways of the world he will witness. The messianic figure is not known by man, and he will be seen in the sky; yet men and women, thought to be intelligent, will be blinded by that which they crave.

A star will be seen and it will move like no other, and the people will gasp and wonder. Fear will fill the heart, yet it need not be filled with that energy... but it is one easily recognised by the heart of man, and brings comfort because it is in their vibration. Yet love will once again sing out over the aeons, and it will bring glory and shine blue for a long period of time.

A little bird will sing its song and be scoffed at, and few will listen... yet the little bird will be protected by one that people will love and admire, and fill other hearts with jealousy. The tall woman will sing the same song, and her light be like no others. The little bird will reach out and still be unheard, until one in a hut will see - and know - and hear its song. Then the little bird will be flying to new heights on the wings of love. But those who wish to steal its treasures will not be able to, because a brilliant light has already told of the one who will steal for greed. So beware, all those that have envy and fear, because it is already known that what lies in the heart cannot be fulfilled, because it is not a righteous desire, but a greedy one based on fear.

That which is laughed at will not be, but it has its journey yet; with good advice given to its participants.

The tulip has a weak stem, but it will be strong once again.

45 north, by east 96, by south 100, with an easterly gale blowing wildly. The men and women will work it out for themselves and want to know more... and why can a bird sing when it is blind, and thought to be talking with eyes that cannot see? Yet the vision will be from a face and heart that can see more than the sight of man.

What is given can be taken, and will be... and it will bring discord, but the fear of the discord will mean that peace will prevail. Not yet my friends... not yet... but it is coming, and the scarred man is working hard with little reward. East by east, and north by the southern seas, and hope will be given.

The journey of that which was thought to be a marvel is corrupt, and will collapse. The collapse is not seen but it will come, because the heart will grow weary and new knowledge will be given.

DO NOT PUT YOUR MONEY INTO THE HANDS OF FOOLS AND GREEDY MEN AND WOMEN, BECAUSE GREED IS NEVER-ENDING.

What is light and bright and travels like no other? It will diminish, if corruption is allowed to grow.

Under the sea... oh 'under the sea' can bring calamity. Avoidance is already in place.

Strong is the heart of man and so is the heart of God, and love will bring both to the light of the universe. It will worm its way into the hope of every fibre, with even the apple having that which it does not want. Yet, hope can still be part of the equation; if the light is seen before it can do what has been planned. Those with no liberty will be barely affected, but the mighty and powerful will be at a loss. Yet this little bird will not be daunted, and will have taken that which it thought is right for its path. Little seeds have already grown, which will not be affected by the worm of the darkened mass in which it lies.
More will come to bring hope. They have no knowledge because

learning is not theirs.

The eagle has flown and is exhausted... its chicks are not ready for what lies ahead.

The spider at the centre is no more, but it has infants who think they are like its guardian, when they are not. They plot and plan with corruption, so they do not understand their own downfall because of it. The deviant is welcomed, but not by the bright light or the lights around it... yet, the light will always welcome, as that is the only way forward.

Nine nines are not always what they seem to be, and the five will outweigh them all.

Powerful, but not yet... awesome, but not in how it is understood today... all will be known nearer the time.

Listen 'Oh those who consider themselves mighty,' for much has been said... Do not look for the obvious, as that is too much and too easy. Consider that which is far from the truth, and then you will know that love is omnipresent. Not yet... not yet... for there is always more... such is the nature of that which is craved and feared. It must stop, and only man can do this... God cannot, for it is not him that wishes for the medicine which pollutes.

The mind will think and the finger will point, and the bringer will have helped the man whose name is one of fear, but it will be good and righteous.

In the small of the night, will the light illuminate and take away - after much hard work - the fear of the east. But is the east 'the east,' or could it be 'the west,' or even 'the north?'

The wall is high and mighty, but not high and mighty enough to prevent the scarred man from rising again.

I laugh, yet I do not... I fear, yet I will never show it... I blow in many directions, and my name is ever a byword for love, under a different guise. On and on, it will roll ever forward... sometimes backwards, but never to the side, as the boulders will prevent it.

Steven is my name and there are many of me, yet I am not one of them.

Fortune favours the brave, but karma has its purpose... and it will play out in a hut, with a bunker of old, and many minds working for the good of mankind. It will go forever - that which plagues every nation, every man and woman - it may not look like it, but man will conquer with many minds together.

I laugh yet I do not, because I am unable... yet 'laughter' is my name, with a cheer or a salute frequently given.

Deep in the forest is a gift not yet given, because it has not been found. Do not destroy the gift, because it can bring hope and a new form of healing.

Atlantis lives, and has never gone, but had to hide over the aeons of time, because its beauty is too much for the heart of man. Now, it will soon be ready to bring good cheer, to the listener with heart to give voice.

With blessings,
from Phoebe.

GOD

MY SONS
(09/04/18 - 11:00)

All three of the men who will now say a little of their stories, are part of the fabric of the early movement, which became known as Christianity. I personally would prefer another name, but I accept what the Earth has chosen. Luke, Matthew, and Paul have a lot to say, and it is about time, as they have been silent for too long. Just as they will ring clear over the years, so will others and I look forward to it immensely. They are sons to me and sons of me, and I thank them for their tireless work and devotion to this world.

At this present time, Matthew and Paul are in Syria; helping where they can… always looking for those in need, and sending love and absent healing to them. Luke is with Jesus in the Halls of Rest, helping men, women, and children from the area known as the 'Near East,' to acclimatise them to their new life in heaven. By this, I mean they are helping the injured, to know that their problems are left with the physical body and do not affect the spiritual one. Some of these injuries are emotional - causing distress - and there are skilled counsellors and healers with Jesus and Luke.

How you treat each other impacts on your arrival to heaven, and the Halls of Rest, and will therefore need the skill of an appropriate spirit plane healer and counsellor. If it is a war situation, then as I am sure you can imagine, a lot of people are required to help the injured, to know they are safe and whole. Food for thought… or so I hope.

Luke, Matthew and Paul have given of their heart and soul, to a lot of Syrian and Iraqi people, who have sought their care and support. They will give to whoever asks and so will I, and all of my sons and daughters.

*****

LUKE

(02/04/18 - 17:02)

I had better say it straight - or at least some of it - but I am not Greek by birth... Egyptian actually, and high-ranking! I was thought to be too much of an individual to be a threat at court, so I was pretty much left to get on with it, until I came to be of an age when I should really have been married.

I always wanted to be a doctor, as the subject fascinated me, and I could see that if you knew what you were doing, you could help. That felt good - being of help - but it was at odds with how a lot of people were at the pharaonic court. Intrigue ruled the day, along with the odd bit of poisoning. I began to see a pattern in men who suddenly died, but said nothing, as I might have ended up that way.

I was miserable as miserable could be... overweight, as I ate too much, and liked dates a great deal. *Who would want to marry me,* I thought... yet a girl was found. She was decent enough, but didn't really like me, as it was to the advantage of her family if we were married. I said 'no,' and that was it... kicked out without as much as a by-your-leave. My family were decent enough to make sure I had enough money, but otherwise it was a case of 'get on with it,' and so I did. I left and never looked back... always forward, sometimes sideways... but never back, unless it was for my safety.

I spread my wings, not really knowing at the same time what to do with my new-found freedom; until I met a Greek physician, who treated me after a case of food poisoning. I told him how much I admired what he did. He looked, said little, and then asked me what I planned to do with the rest of my life... if I didn't kill myself first from gluttony. I felt fit-for-nothing, well-educated maybe, but aimless... no direction or inspiration. 'Teach me' I suddenly said, and he did. I could go into it more, but that is enough, as he got me on the path of the straight and narrow, until my life turned another corner.

I will always be grateful to this man, who saw something in me which I didn't. He saw my potential and never gave up on me, when I floundered or lost confidence. My story with Jesus and others like him is for another day, when time has unfolded, so that which seems impossible suddenly isn't. So until then, remember that the twists and turns of life sometimes are for a reason, and at the time, we don't always know why.

*****

MATTHEW

(03/04/18 - 17:36)

Like Luke, I was pretty miserable with my lot in life, apart from my wife and daughters. I loved them very much and they loved me in the same way. It didn't stop me though, from feeling disgusted with myself and my line of work... very little helped, until I met Jesus.

He never judged me, as he saw that I did that myself; but it was in his nature and understanding not to. My journey with him was a momentous one, which changed my life entirely. I left my work and gave a lot of money away - much to the anger of my parents - and felt better for it. I wasn't a tax collector, but what I did still disgusted me, and I couldn't see my way out. Yet Jesus did, he told me that all I had to do was look forward, and trust, not only in God, but myself. Now, trusting my own judgment was a difficult path to walk, but I tried to do as he said... not because it was him, but I saw the merit and sense of it. How was I ever going to leave the clutches of being an informant for the highest bidder, if I personally didn't do something about it?

It was a lucrative way of life, as I had dipped my fingers into other avenues, but I had felt for a long time that my cheating and swindling was making me ill... Ill in mind, body, and soul. I was morbidly obese, walked with a limp - as I had a very sore big toe - and was depressed. Yet, Jesus saw the light of my soul, and knew that if I answered his call, I would walk a different path with joy in my heart. It wasn't easy - far from it - but I felt so much better, and I have never regretted a single moment of my life since.

I have many years before *Skylark* decides to finish with the writing, so I don't have to explain everything at once. I think what I have said so far might just be enough for starters. You can see that how I earned my daily bread wasn't something to be proud of, and that I had fingers in more than one pie; which involved some degree of swindling... which meant I had to lie, frequently. I became a reformed man and felt free for the first time in my life, and for that I have Jesus to thank.

*****

PAUL

(09/04/18 - 10:34)

The story of part of my life, and conversion, in the New Testament is right with one thing… and that is… I was an ultra-religious Jew. I knew how many steps I took each Sabbath, and by the time I was a young man I was ill because of it, and starting to develop a lot of strange habits and mannerisms. Matthew and his family helped me in more ways than you can imagine, and I thank him from the bottom of my heart for his generosity and hospitality.

I was a broken man when I turned up at the community where Matthew lived. He took me in and shielded me from the world, until I could look at it again. I had just witnessed the crucifixion of a female apostle of Jesus'. It was such a terrible thing to have seen, so much so, that it tipped me over the edge. I had liked and respected her, you see. I couldn't openly say it at the time, but her voice rang clear whenever she spoke, and I wanted to be there at the end of her life. Not to gloat - far from it - but to support her with my prayers.

When I walked away from the abomination and injustice I had just experienced, I thought I would never recover, and regain some semblance of my life. So I did the only thing I could think of, and walked to where Matthew lived, and broke down in front of him. That was the beginning of my so called 'Damascus conversion', and it was a journey which could fill more than one book.

I have, of course, spoken to *Skylark* about it, and about my life and time with Matthew, but there is always more… and more on top of that, as I lived to a ripe old age and beyond; with children and grandchildren. I knew Adu and Deborah, Phoebe and Luke, and a great many other workers of the early movement. I lived in Africa and Europe and helped in Rome. So, you can see I have a lot to say, and so do Luke and Matthew.

We are nothing special in the grand scheme of it all, as there were more than us; but if you can accept our truths, then it will help you to understand others. Phoebe was eloquent in her prophetic state, and Deborah, a tall strong woman whose voice reached hundreds, when she spoke.

It is a journey for us to tell you, of our comings and goings... and a different kind of one for you, because you will be challenged, shocked, and surprised in the nicest of ways... or so we hope!

With blessings to you all,
Paul.

DENNIS POTTER

WHY DID I ASK FOR IT?
(10/04/18 - 10:25)

When I died, I wondered where I was. It was far beyond what I ever imagined... dying that is! Much easier than I had anticipated, but then again, I had help from a lovely soul called Magdalene.

She told me that I would speak again, and I thought her far-fetched... now look and see what's what. I am speaking again through a medium called *Skylark*, and that I never could have imagined, or written about. My wife is close by and I have, of course, asked her if there is anything she particularly wants me to say. We have chatted about one or two things, and I have spoken to *Skylark,* to say that I plan to talk about my experience with psoriasis and psoriatic arthritis. You see I can say things that *Skylark* can't, and I have told her that too. Of course it has made her wonder what I am going to talk about, and what the dermatologist is going to say after me... nice man, Doctor Munro, and I am glad to have made his acquaintance. He has helped me in a lot of ways, as I have been able to talk to him extensively about this tricky condition, known as 'psoriasis.'

I asked my guide Ruth, *'why did I have to suffer like I did?',* and she replied, *'well Dennis, you asked for it as part of your life experience.'* That, I didn't expect! It never entered my head that I could have asked for suffering as part of the progression of my soul.

It was a dreadful experience at times, and that's before I even begin on the desire to scratch myself silly. *How on Earth could I have asked for it?* I pondered this question a lot, and always *why oh why couldn't I have chosen something different?* I have understood more now, after my time in spirit, and I can say that 'I get it!' I asked for the skin and bone experience, so that I would understand the suffering of others, as part of internal and spiritual growth. It made me feel cranky at times, if I am honest, and when I wrote it gave me some sort of space or time, away from how I was feeling. I think the pain clouded my judgement, and in the long-term affected my character, as I could never seem to get on top of it... especially in the joints.

I lived with pain - pretty much - for a long period of time, but there was pain I could tolerate and put to the back of my mind, and on other occasions - when in a flare-up - I could never escape from it. It was exhausting, if I am honest, and I am sorry for every single person who has it. Yet, there are a lot of delightful men, women, and children that smile at the world, get on with their lives, and accept who they are and what they have, and I applaud them for it... I wish I could have been more like that!

Now, what I am going to say is my opinion only, and nothing to do with *Skylark*. She is just the conduit through which I wish to speak my mind... so, do not blame the messenger, as it is not her fault! Psoriasis is underfunded! Ha, but then again so are a lot of things in this age of cuts and austerity. *Why bother about funny-looking skin, which can make you itch, compared to cancer or heart disease?* Why bother indeed... because it is one of the worst things I experienced in my life as Dennis Potter! That's before I even begin on the treatment I was given, which affected my day-to-day living.

Psoriasis goes beyond the skin, as it can potentially affect every bone in your body, your heart and lungs... and all from a little itch that looks a bit red, white, and scaly. *A bit scaly!* Well... when I used to undress it was a like a snowstorm in our bedroom! My wife deserved a medal for just sharing a room with me; never mind our comfortable bed, because of how my skin used to bleed. I often despaired, but hid it, as I couldn't let people see how I really felt. My clothes also used to act as a form of loofah against my skin, making it all worse. Even when I walked, I found myself leaving a trail, when the psoriasis was bad. So you can see, how when I was told about this gift I had chosen, I thought myself mad. Mad as the proverbial March hare!

I do not feel like that anymore, and have accepted myself and in doing so, my understanding of the condition is different. Perhaps though, you can begin to understand that I am angry at how psoriasis is brushed under the carpet, as if it is nothing! It is more than what you think it is, and a lot of people have it in varying forms and degrees. It is a disease of the mind, body, and soul... and treated as something to be ignored.

DOCTOR MUNRO

BRUSHED UNDER THE CARPET
(10/04/18 - 11:15)

When I was a medical student, I spent some time in the dermatology department of the hospital I trained at. It was time well spent, as I felt I could be of help and service. I could see the suffering of the people in clinic, and how relieved they were when help was given. I also saw the results of coal tar paste and Dithranol, UVB and coal tar baths, and emollients given to help moisturise the skin. I knew that I could help a lot of people, if I specialised in this area, so I decided to do just that.

I was a consultant dermatologist at Saint Bartholomew's Hospital in London, the Royal Masonic Hospital, and I attended one or two others. I never regretted the decision I made to specialise in skin disease, but times are different now, and I personally think it is more difficult for outpatient clinics in dermatology. There were always beds available at Saint Bartholomew's Hospital, when I felt that a person was in such a condition that they required my team to take over, and help them get to a state where they were - to my mind - socially acceptable, and able to feel more comfortable with their skin.

If a young woman turned up at clinic covered from head to toe, itching beyond what she could tolerate, and the psoriasis was highly visible, I felt compelled to do nothing but admit her, and take over the treatment to help her find relief. Do not think me a cruel man when I say the words 'socially unacceptable,' but that is how I felt when things were so bad that my team and I had to take over, because the psoriasis was getting out of control.

To my mind, psoriasis is a condition that *should* be accepted by society, no matter its state, but it is not because people do not understand what it is like or how it feels. It can and does affect the self-esteem of a lot of individuals, so I do not use the words I have said lightly.

I agree with Dennis Potter that it is underfunded; partly because it is not 'fashionable,' is misunderstood and easily ignored. Yet, if I were to tell you that waiting in the ethers to be discovered, is a form of treatment that is hugely beneficial and with little side effects, how would that make you, the reader, feel? I know how I feel, and Dennis has told me what he thinks about it. It is a joy, waiting for an inquisitive soul to discover. It won't go down well in some areas, because it could lower revenue, as it has immense potential in the long run.

A condition like psoriasis deserves some focus from our current medical departments. Imagine having it on your face so badly that you can barely smile? I have seen it like that, so perhaps you are starting to get some idea of its possible spread to areas that are highly troublesome. Imagine having more than one skin condition on your face? We live in a world obsessed with beauty, yet there was beauty inside every person I treated with psoriasis... still, they could have been judged in an unfair contest, whereby their inner soul was not seen for its quality and potential. Having the condition, psoriasis, is nothing about the fairness of life, but it does not mean that we doctors cannot treat with the same equality and knowledge, that we give to other patients. Many a doctor in general practice is under-funded and over-worked, the same as in our busy hospitals.

Because psoriasis is rarely a life-threatening illness, it is overlooked in the scheme of things... but it is a lifelong condition with emotional consequences. Not for all, and I accept that, but our feelings of self-worth, in an age of photos being enhanced, so the individual looks leaner or has a much clearer skin, does not help when dealing with conditions which can be highly visible. Let your real beauty shine through, and then look again, and you will all see differently, the picture in front of you!

*****

MATTHIAS

A DOORKEEPER'S PERSPECTIVE
(10/04/18 - 14:56)

Good afternoon, my name is Matthias and I am *Skylark's* doorkeeper. *Skylark* has just asked me a question, partly out of mischief, but also fairness and managing the link. I like this mischievous side to *Skylark,* because she said it with a little laugh at the same time… and I can tell from her vibration that it is nothing of ill will. As this is an appropriate way for a guide or doorkeeper to answer a question, then it is right that I do so, here and now. The answer is *'Rachel',* and for you to know the question, you had better ask *Skylark* when you can… if you are interested, that is.

I have been *Skylark's* doorkeeper for many lives, so I know her quite well. Some of the lives were male, but in spirit, vibration is more important than gender. To her friends, *Skylark* can appear as energy, but if the need is there, then the female form is taken. This is because *Skylark* also works in her sleep state, in the spirit plane. Not every night, as there are times when we work on her etheric template, to aid her wellbeing, so she can complete the book and feel better in the process. That is why there are gaps in the line of letters, as the spiritual pathway is about balance. If *Skylark* is busy or feeling unwell, then we never push the writing or encourage her to write. It would be ungodly of any doorkeeper, or guide, to behave in such a manner! All of us are there for the good of *Skylark,* and not for our own personal motives. We are with her to teach and inspire.

I am the main guide, along with Rachel, as we are the most experienced. Rachel is a sister-of-mercy and a most illumined soul, who has been with *Skylark* all of her life. Unlike the other guides who will come and go, as *Skylark* grows in understanding, Rachel will be constant, along with me.

A person's doorkeeper *always* will be the same spirit plane soul, because they are in charge of the other guides. The other guides are like teachers… when a new and deeper understanding is needed, then a different guide steps in. Think of it like teachers in a school and changing classes each year, and you will get the gist of it. One difference though, is that a person will rarely change guides yearly, because there is a lot each one has to offer, and it can take a long time before you outgrow your guide. *Skylark* will never outgrow Rachel or me, because we are too evolved for that, but she is making good headway, and we are very proud of her and her determination to carry on, when others might step back.

You see, the young woman Doctor Munro spoke of in his letter, with uncontrollable psoriasis, was *Skylark,* when she was a much younger woman; barely out of her teens. She was considered by him to be socially unacceptable, as the psoriasis on her scalp was creeping down onto her face, and the itch all over her body was getting to her. It is at the moment, if I am honest! Even Rachel and I have to agree with that, as we can tell how troublesome it is. I know *Skylark* doesn't mind, but I won't say too much, as that is for her at the right time… if she ever wants to. So, we try when she is asleep, to help, and often at night she falls asleep in front of the television, because of the healing we channel to her. Fortunately for us, she doesn't mind, and understands because of the help we give… especially as she has psoriatic arthritis, like Dennis had. So, the gaps in the letters are mainly down to her wellbeing. Rachel is with *Skylark,* as she is a skilled reader of the etheric template, and had the same conditions as *Skylark* in a previous life… so her understanding is a deep one.

I want to make one thing crystal clear, and this is that, we never disturb *Skylark*… ever… or butt in when she is in conversation, or pester her when she is in bed. All of you take note, as *no guide should behave in such a way*… and if one ever did, then speak to a skilled person on their spiritual pathway, who can help you.

Sometimes people are enthusiastic in the early days of learning about their pathway, without having the understanding of what is spiritually right or wrong. Your guide taking over, or being pushy, or living their life through you is non-negotiable. I wouldn't want a guide like that around me, and neither would *Skylark*. So, remember that you are always in control not your guide. The same goes for spirit plane communicators, as it is your life and not theirs, so they should never tell you what to do or disturb your sleep; wake you up, or do anything of such a nature.

If you want to walk your pathway, learn about mediumship or how to channel the healing energy... it is vital that you do, so you manage your linking and not spirit. That way you will have greater control and understand what is right or wrong, and not be pestered by troublesome communicators. *Skylark* had to learn and so did Rachel.

If you have questions about spirit, or any aspect of the spirit plane, answers can come in all sorts of ways, and writing like this is one of them. Another is to ask a soul, skilled like Isaiah Abbotsbury, or someone like him. Perhaps you have a question about guides? Well, maybe Alex can hopefully answer in his letter... queries floating in the ether... or maybe I have answered them in this one.

You may find a book with an answer, or even in an address from a medium, during a service in a spiritualist church. So, there are a few appropriate ways, and of course others that are not so good... I personally would never recommend a Ouija board, as that could be an open portal... difficult to close. I know that *Skylark* agrees with me.

She doesn't like the cabinet, and thinks that, in the wrong hands, is an open portal too... I can't say that it is a favourite of mine, because I can see a lot more about entities in the cabinet, than any leader of a group can. Perhaps these are two ways to avoid open communication with a spirit plane individual. Note, I say 'individual,' because you are hardly likely to get a high level soul connect with either of these tools... the opposite is more like it!

Sometimes we do things out of enthusiasm, and it can land us in a bit of a pickle, spiritually speaking. Your guides will always help you, as will your doorkeeper... but it is never your doorkeeper's responsibility, if you do something out of freewill. Help will always be given, but the choice is down to the individual. That is why 'choice' is always a personal thing, if communication is given from a loved-one in spirit. *The medium, of course, needs to understand the importance of not giving communication, which tells a person what to do, what to buy, or how to live their life.*
That is why the repeal of the Fraudulent Mediums Act, in the United Kingdom, was a good thing, when it happened not many years

ago*. It means that mediums are responsible for the messages they give, so the communicators have to buck-up and learn what is acceptable and what isn't, to say to a loved one. On the other hand, a person cannot expect a medium to tell them what to do. If you don't know which house to buy, then how do you expect a deceased person to know? If put like that, it makes sense, because we have the karma of our lives to consider, and freewill, which is important.

So, if any of you are planning to visit a medium in the United Kingdom, for a reading, do not turn up expecting to be given answers to things that you have the responsibility for. Neither *Skylark* nor Isaiah will give you the answer to whom you should marry, which house or car to buy, or the job to go for, as they understand the responsibility of the Fraudulent Mediums Act. Besides, they respect their gifts too much, and have worked too hard to go down the fortune-telling route. What they will bring through for you is evidence of your loved one, how they are doing, and what they would like to say.

Skylark's mother recently came through, via Isaiah, talking about her bunions. It was evidence of her mother, and the state of her feet on the Earth, but then she followed it with how she was doing and how her understanding was changing, which was important for *Skylark* to hear. Simple it may sound, yet important, as it meant that *Skylark's* mother was healing on an emotional level, and able to talk about things she couldn't before.

It is not unusual for an angry parent or relative to begin to heal, when they are shown love and respect. They can then start to see how things could have been different, and are even able to say 'sorry' to a friend or relative they mistreated. *Readings do not have to be about anything other than love, support, and guidance... which allows for personal responsibility and it can allow for healing on both levels of consciousness.*

I have been a doorkeeper for a lot of lives, and David Bowie once said to *Skylark,* that if I opened my aura up, it could scare a lot of unwanted souls away. He may be right, but that isn't always the best way to go about matters... sometimes learning the importance of how to link with the spirit plane is too important, not to have an unwanted experience, if it is on your pathway to be a teacher.

We can learn by our mistakes; stumble and fall, but our inner strength means we can pick ourselves up again and remember the lesson... and that could be one thing off the karmic 'tick list' for the current life.

It was like this for Rachel in one of her lives... and I hasten to add, it upset her dreadfully, yet she understood, and made sure that any students she had, knew the value of managing the link with guides and communicators. Sometimes it is our own inexperience, or even just what happens when a grumpy soul knocks on our door, spiritually speaking. I cannot stress enough that *if you walk your path, you have to understand a lot of the theory of what to do, when, and how.* It is not up to me or any other doorkeeper to do that for you. Sorry if I sound a little hard, but people misunderstand what a doorkeeper is, so I had better explain a little of it...

A doorkeeper is a very experienced guide, who is the manager of 'karmic opportunities' upon a person's pathway. This will also involve 'karmic choice,' as something may crop up, previously agreed to, and pass by. This has happened once already for *Skylark*... which was learning calligraphy. It was a difficult subject for her, unlike her talented mother, who teaches this subject in the Halls of Learning... so, for now, *Skylark* has let this go.

Doorkeepers are also in charge of the other guides, because of the level of experience they have. A doorkeeper is there to watch and help the individual, organise healing for them, from their guides - when the need is there - and encourage the communicators, if a medium is serving a church. I also allow *Skylark's* family and friends to help me with this, when she takes a service, as they are very keen and are also friendly.... I can see the value of allowing them to help me. Yet, I hasten to add; they are not guides and never will be. They work with me because *I allow them to,* and for no other reason. They do not butt in and interfere, as I would stop them, and alert *Skylark* to this fact, so she could also step in and take charge. We work as a team, but it still means that the character of the communicator will come through.

On one occasion, *Skylark* felt that a communicator was trying to boss her about. This was evidence of the person's mother, as they were a little domineering on the Earth. On another, she felt a grandfather energy draw near... he was a nice, gentle man, and tried to help *Skylark* as much as he could, while she gave the communication to his granddaughter... and this was felt too. So, you can see the variety of loved ones who come through to give a message.

The teamwork which I speak of is on all levels of consciousness, because we have guides who are there for the guides, if a situation is very difficult for the person on the Earth. We also have someone to turn to, if we need it. So far we have not, because everything has turned out as planned, despite the difficulties *Skylark* has faced on her karmic path. The guides' guide for us is a delightful man, called Peter. He also acts as a spiritual auditor, and looks in from time to time anyway, to see that all is well. He is always keen for a bit of a chat, and even turned up in time for a painting session, so somewhere in a large box, is a painting of Peter in his etheric form and vibration.

This will be different to what Vincent van Gogh will eventually do, but he has been busy doing night skies with *Skylark,* and will soon begin a series of paintings of the northern lights with her. It was *Skylark's* request to do this, and Vincent is well and truly up for it, in the most positive of ways, as he can see more than most in the way of colour in the sky. This means that the paintings she does may be vivid, because that is what Vincent sees in the energy of the northern lights. However it may begin with lots of green and dashes of pink... but that I leave for him to sort out, as it is his role with Rachel, or I, close by in attendance.

I could go on and on, but I know that I have to leave space for Alex and other communicators. We still have Cary Grant to look forward to, a couple more kings, and a delightful gardener called Percy Thrower; along with God, Judas Iscariot, Levi, and an author, whose work *Skylark* likes.

As for me, I like my work and role, and have done it many times; learning as much as I can to help me in the next life. I am a middle-aged man from the Lebanon... tall for the times, in this persona... you couldn't pull the wool over my eyes back then, and you can't now! I have seen it all, so nothing surprises me... not even war and conflict! I feel saddened by war though, yet I can't let it affect my role, or the healing energy I channel to the people of Iraq and Syria.

They were in *Skylark's* prayers during the service on Sunday, which she took, and are frequently in her absent healing book's list of names to pray for. So, when she thinks of all the names in her book, we guides do to, and her family join us… it is a blessing and a joy to be of service to you!

*   ***The Fraudulent Mediums Act 1951*** *was a law in England and Wales, which   prohibited a person from claiming to be a **psychic**, **medium,** or other **spiritualist,**   while attempting to deceive and to make money from the deception (other than solely for the purpose of entertainment). It repealed the **Witchcraft Act 1735,** and it was, in turn, repealed on **26th May 2008,** by new **Consumer Protection Regulations;** following an EU directive, targeting unfair sales and marketing practices.*

*****

ALEX

NOW A GUIDE'S
(14/04/18 - 13:12)

I don't want you to think that I am going to go over what my friend and teacher Matthias has just said, because I am not about to do anything of the sort. We may have one or two experiences which are similar, as I have been a guide to *Skylark* before, so I know her quite well too. The difference is that I have not done it as many times as Matthias, so he has the experience of lives which I do not.

So, my name is Alex… I am a young monk in age, but from level four of the spirit plane; which means my understanding is greater than most upon the Earth. My age in spirit is of no consequence because of my vitality, karma, and understanding of the philosophy of life. I have been with *Skylark* for a few years now, and will not be moving for some time yet. It is not because I have so much knowledge; it is precisely the kind that I do have, which makes my role 'as long as it takes.' I am on good terms with Benedict (saint by that name, upon the Earth) and Mother Teresa, and I get on well with Rose and Judas Iscariot. So, now some of my credentials are out of the way I can begin, as they say.

I enjoy what I do, which is a good thing, as it would make my role difficult if I didn't. *Skylark* is always in control and I understand that and its importance, because if I didn't then I think I would be booted out; taken to one side by Peter and asked what on Earth I thought I was doing. After that it would be a karmic so-called kick in the teeth for me… in the nicest of ways, I am sure. Still, the end result would mean that I would never be a guide again. If you didn't understand what Matthias meant in his letter, then maybe now you do. Sometimes we do repeat ourselves in spirit, if giving an understanding, because if it's not retained in one way, then it might be in another.

Part of my role is to help *Skylark* in the development of her mediumship. She has had at least three previous lives, of which she had mediumistic ability and ignored it, and a great deal more, in which she used it in one way or the other. This means that writing with her guides is not new to her, because if it was she would not have the likes of Winston Churchill or Benjamin Disraeli penning a letter. It has taken lives of practice and karma to get to this point. The same for Isaiah Abbotsbury; he would not be interested in them if he was new to it all. A new soul will take little interest, or else for the less enlightened of reasons, and an older soul will sit up and pay attention; which is what he and Tilly do. *Skylark* does not remote scan or is a seer, yet she will see into many things which is godly of origin, but it has not started yet... so let's not get excited about that one (as it is something to go whoopee about). Isaiah will have different things on his spiritual plate, which I will not name.

I have been with *Skylark* while Isaiah is guiding her, in how to do readings and past-life regression, and when she is asking questions about mediumship or channelling; as that forms part of my teaching role. I do not interfere, yet I can intuitively help. I am also present when the communicators step in to give a letter, as I enjoy the process... so I can tell you one or two things about that.

They always send absent healing to *Skylark* while doing their letter. They are asked to by *Skylark's* mother, because she has now realised what her daughter has endured over the years, and wishes to help and not hinder. I am also asked at the same time - and it is another aspect of my role - to send absent healing and help Rachel, when she is scanning the etheric template of *Skylark's* aura. Rachel is doing this more and more. *Skylark* knows when it is being recalibrated, because she feels a little jolt and will often feel energy running though her body, along one of the meridians. Not all the time, as sometimes Rachel will do it metaphysically. Then *Skylark* will feel nothing but the end result, when it is released. I say 'released' as big changes are coming and they cannot come all at once; so bit by bit, with a nicely impatient *Skylark* telling us to hurry up, they are slowly coming.

The different communicators can see when Rachel is working, so sometimes they ask if they can send absent healing. Matthias stands by, in his doorkeeper role, at the time, because Rachel has a strong focus which cannot be diverted away from the etheric template. If Rachel is free she will say 'yes', otherwise Matthias will agree. We know the calibre of the communicators, and you cannot pull the wool over Matthias' or Rachel's eyes. *Skylark* does not need to give agreement to this here and now, because it was given in spirit before she reincarnated; as the recalibration of the etheric template is part of her karma. Both Rachel and Matthias know this, as they discussed *Skylark's* life and karma with her prior to reincarnation.

Now, back to the letters and communicators! I am not alone as Matthias is here, along with *Skylark's* twin sister Samantha, and their mother and brothers... and of course a few family pets, which are important, as animals can channel the healing energy the same as humans... so, a nice little family unit, while I am doing my letter. Sometimes the communicators will show *Skylark* something... it's very rare that happens, but it has.

Alan Rickman showed himself in conversation with Christopher Hitchins, before one piece of writing. Christopher looked to be regaling Alan about one of his exploits here on the Earth, and the two men were getting on. When *Skylark* spoke to Isaiah and Tilly about Adu's letter, he showed himself deep in conversation with his friend Paul (apostle of that name). They were in Africa, sitting outside by the fire one evening, and Paul's cloak was the blue of the African sky at night. Elijah, as you know, portrayed himself one hot day, deep in a cave. *Skylark* has seen a current keeper of the records of the history of church with a parchment in front of him, whilst explaining to another man what it said. Now, that was neither of them doing that, as it was given clairvoyantly, to show *Skylark* one of the consequences of the letters. That's just some of the experiences so far, and I could say more, but enough for the time being, as I have other things to talk about.

As a guide, I am constantly learning. You wouldn't expect a solicitor or teacher not to keep updated, so it's the same for the guides. I can go to the Halls of Learning, for example, if a skilled doorkeeper is giving a teaching session on an aspect of this role. I will eventually learn enough to undertake the role of a doorkeeper for a future Earth plane soul. *Skylark* had a guide from India, called Jasmine, who has now moved on and is teaching in the Halls of Learning. With more experience she will eventually become a doorkeeper for one very lucky Earth individual or individuals... you ask *Skylark* how hard she worked in her role as guide, with her. A very lovely lady indeed, is Jasmine!

Matthias will also teach as he goes along, as does Rachel,

especially if she has just worked on the etheric template. It was 'all hands on deck' a few years ago when *Skylark* had a flare up with the psoriatic arthritis and psoriasis, which resulted in PUVA (ultraviolet light therapy) and then surgery. Rachel couldn't do as much as she wanted to back then, because this aspect of suffering was part of the karma of *Skylark's* path. Absent healing was sent, but the flare-up had to be gone through, and managed by Earth clinicians and not spirit plane ones.

That is important too, as we in spirit are never the person's doctor, dentist, physiotherapist, or other such individual. Rachel might be working on *Skylark's* etheric template, but she still had to see her doctor and a physiotherapist, because her back was having problems in January, February and March of this year... the exercises given by the physiotherapist are still being done. So, what's the point, and why now is the etheric template being worked on by Rachel and Judas Iscariot? Judas is a highly-skilled soul, who will help Rachel as and when demanded. Just because his reputation isn't great, it doesn't mean to say that he is not... and he is! So, when asked, he helps. Anyway, why now? Matthias may have touched on it in his piece, when he said it was to help *Skylark* finish the book, and help her feel better in the process. Yet it is more than that, as this is the first of many books which *Skylark* will transcribe, and if we do not help it may, or may not, be the only one. Such is the nature of a chronic health condition, and that's before I even begin on the tiredness. So, on that note *Skylark* says we are done for today (remember she manages the link, not I).

Until we begin again, with blessings to you all
Alex

...Once again, we kick off a couple of days later; one sunny afternoon, after *Skylark* is getting over another hiccup in her wellbeing. It may not have lasted long, but it was enough to prevent her from writing, so perhaps you can see why we need to do something to help.

So, where was I... the etheric template? Well, I think I have said enough on that, so I will commence a new subject, which might make you sit up and pay attention, or scoff at it...

You can all do it you know - write with your guide that is - but you have to know how to go about it, so it's done correctly. Now, don't blame me if you go off and give it a go, and get it wrong! Many a keen person has done that, only to end up writing for hours or nothing at all. *It's always best to write with your development circle leader first, until you build up confidence, so he or she can explain what to do, how long to write for, and on what topic. If you don't, you could potentially end up opening your spiritual door to the wrong kind of communicator… and that none of us would want!* A development circle can also be called 'an open circle' because it is open to everyone to attend.

Skylark sat for twenty minutes and did four passive meditations, prior to starting this letter again. Now, you don't have to do that, but she understands the importance of her personal development, and making sure the link is up and running; so the words are received as clearly and precisely as possible. The four are important for her mediumship development, and worked well to tune up the crown chakra, prior to *'you know who'* getting going again. *Skylark* writes on her own, and could even teach it to new people if she felt like it… but she doesn't, so won't be doing that for a while yet (well-being again).

This isn't the first draft of the book, or even the first book, as there are quite a few 'practice' books, to build up the knowledge. It was important for her to get used to writing with apostles, so she wouldn't be put off when it came to the real thing. The same as personalities; as there is one communicator who must have penned at least sixty pieces, if not more, so it makes no difference to her who it is. She is not flustered or impressed, and that is how we like it. So, when Jesus recently wrote with her privately, she bellowed something out, after she realised she had 'drifted off' mid-piece and begun to think about something else. He wasn't bothered, and quite likes a bit of individuality… so does God, as he has communicated before this second draft, which did cause a little bit of excitement… especially when the stiff hands and fingers flew across the keyboard, after Judas said that the spirit of the Lord was upon him. Oh the joys of writing!

So before I start another topic, I need to encourage you to write with your guide… but *you have to be taught by someone who knows how to do it… I can't stress enough the importance of that!* Most spiritualist churches have at least one person they could refer you to; or even have teachers at the church, with development groups that can show you what to do, and guide you in the process.

The open circle *Skylark* attends has a teacher who knows what's what. There are others in the United Kingdom to go to, but not all have a writing focus; so check first or go anyway, and see if you enjoy it. If you don't, then find another that you feel comfortable in. This is also important, because if you enjoy the energy of the development group (or open circle), then you will learn more and make friends in the process.

Both Matthias and I have spoken about you managing your pathway - and being in charge - and not the guides. *Now I want to touch on balance; because the spiritual pathway isn't all 'spirit' and not going out... it is about both, and doing the grocery shopping, organising a wedding, reading a novel and going clothes shopping.* It is about the whole of life, because if your pathway was so focused on the material, the spiritual side could be dim and distant. The other way around, would mean that working with your guides was the priority, when there are friends to be had, and fun with them. So, make sure that yours is about balance, if you decide to put your toe in the water, spiritually speaking.

It is for *Skylark,* and is about to open up even further, on the material and spiritual. The same for Isaiah Abbotsbury and his wife Tilly. Changes are coming for them too, along with a planned holiday, so both get some rest, and a bit of fun and excitement. Everything about the spirit side of life is to be enjoyed, but I think when *Skylark* has finished this book, she will take a break and that's good... balance, as I say!

Now, something else I would like to add before I sign off... which is *Skylark* doesn't consider herself religious; neither does she go down the route of 'sin and obedience.' You could consider that unusual, or else see it as okay, but it's true! Sin and obedience do not figure in her life. She doesn't consider herself a sinner, nor anybody else. She might wonder about one or two people, whose shoes she wouldn't want to be in, because of the news and what is portrayed... but she also understands that she doesn't know the full picture, and that personal responsibility is what so-called 'sin' is about.

What you might consider a sin, I might not, and vice versa... except that I don't 'do' sin either! Too much about blame, and blame for what? How can you claim to be a sinner without saying what you think it is that you have done? Is it up to any person on this Earth to judge you, if you confess your sin? Nobody can forgive on the behalf of someone else. God can't forgive the sin of another... he can only forgive wrongdoing against him.

Jesus may have been thought to have died for our sins, but if he had been crucified, I don't think it would have been sin he was dying for. I hope I haven't upset any of you by saying that, but I can't lie, and to some extent the church is based upon a misunderstanding. A misunderstanding of love, but love is still with each and every one of you... even if the basis of the early movement is different to what has been taught. It is far more about love than you realise, but love with no judgement or sin attached to it... and no obedience either!

Marcus never judged another person in Rome that asked for help, no matter what they did, and neither did Camilla. If she had, then a man called Demetrius would never have had the experience he did, after she left him one hot day. Karma does not judge, it acts in the only way it knows - through impartiality - and the healing energy channelled is the same.

We judge ourselves, and are far more harsh and critical than God. Of course, there are men and women whose acts are despicable. They think they can get away with it, but can't; and it is not through the judgement meted out by God, but through the impartiality of karma.

So, remember that love is uppermost in the heart of God, but the way to him is not solely Christian. It is every way that makes the heart sing, when goodness and joy is part of the equation of life.

*****

156

VINCENT VAN GOGH

A NIGHT TO REMEMBER
(19/04/18 - 08:06)

You all know how much I liked to paint so I won't pretend otherwise, but what you don't know is that I frequently saw the aura around inanimate objects, and in the night sky. Sometimes the colours were subtle, and other times not, as it depended on what was happening at the time. Now, I can't prove this to you and neither can Isaiah or *Skylark*, but I wouldn't be surprised at some of you being able to see what I saw. It fuelled my painting, so maybe when you see one with lots of colour you might guess at what inspired me.

I will paint with *Skylark*, officially, but for now it's unofficial, because she wouldn't show anyone, apart from Tilly, what we have done together so far. Now, I am not an unkind man, but David Bowie is correct in what he said earlier... we do have a long way to go before either of us is pleased. I am not judging *Skylark,* but I am her guide and inspirer for the painting, and that only. So I want to uplift and encourage as much as I can, and am not happy until I feel I have done that to the best of my ability. As for *Skylark*, it is a journey and her ability is dormant, but it will surface. Yet it doesn't mean that I cannot see her potential, because I do, and you will too when she is much older... and it might be a surprise. If you think this is all a fabrication that is up to you but none in spirit lie ever... unless of course you are in the lower levels, experiencing the karma of what you gave to your fellow man. Then the lies flow fast and furious, yet are never believed, as the aura gives too much away to the experienced souls, who give of their hearts to the - as yet - unenlightened.

I have painted lots of night skies in my time, as I have continued here in spirit and with *Skylark*. We have painted together the etheric form of one or two of her guides, and will paint Marcus and Camilla, side by side, again in the same way. *Skylark* would like Marcus and Camilla's painting to go into the book, because of how she feels about them. All we can do is see what Isaiah says. If they are not included, then maybe later on you will get a glimpse of two of the most beautiful souls I have ever met.

I don't like theft, so I am not happy that some of my work was stolen. Neither am I pleased that my paintings could fetch ridiculous amounts of money. I do not want them bought as a trophy. I want all of my work enjoyed, and not what they may or may not be potentially worth at auction, or privately. It is my opinion only, which I know doesn't count, because if it did then that would be worrying, to not only me but my guide Rosanna. I am allowed to say what I wish, and that is how I feel at this present moment (things change just as the seasons do).

On the subject of David Bowie, his artwork is coming on nicely, and his style is taking shape and form. He is not alone, as not only am I teaching him, but also a great many souls wishing to learn, and give of their heart in their creativity. I applaud them all, and find great joy in this.

To begin with, when I first arrived in heaven, I didn't want to paint. I felt distorted within myself and angry that life continued... so angry at that! I wanted the flurry of my mind to stop and go away... yet it had! I didn't know because I was too bound up with what I thought was going on, without realising that the reality was far different. I was free of everything that I wished to be, yet clung on because it was what I knew. I was fearful of life, so I held onto the Earth reality, and not my healed spirit one.

My guide Rosanna tried to help, and then she asked a man called Malcolm, from the Halls of Rest, to speak to me. It was the best thing she could have done, as I didn't listen to her, yet I did to him; because it felt that he somehow knew what I had gone through, and did not judge me for my actions. I am blessed with having Rosanna as my guide, but I didn't know it back then, as my mind and judgement were clouded... it took Malcolm to show me the new reality of where I was.

One of the other things I do, besides painting, is to try to help people like me. I will go and talk to anybody when I am asked to. Always there are questions, which I don't mind, because I answer to the best of my ability, and hope it brings a new reality which uplifts the soul.

So, until we meet again through colour and vitality,
Adieu

GEORGE (the THIRD of that name)

THEY GOT IT ALL WRONG
(21/04/18 - 16:20)

I was not mentally unstable! I want to make this clear from the start. If I was, then I wouldn't be now, because of the vibration of the spirit plane, and everything we who live here are offered. I am fed up with being thought of as 'mad King George, who lost the colonies,' and would quite like it if history could tell a different story... I could... I could tell you many a thing about my family of dissolute sons. A bag of ragamuffins the lot, but the worst was my eldest and namesake. He was a fornicator, thief and liar... and that is just for starters! However, I would like to say a little more about my illness.

I am not a bitter man - do not ever think it - but the doctors back then were the biggest bunch of quacks you could come across. I should know, as I was treated by a few of them. I felt so ill at times, and couldn't make anybody understand what I was feeling. They were baffled and put it down to insanity... no doubt encouraged by my son and heir. Typical I suppose, of the relationship between Hanoverian sons and fathers. I died feeling like an abandoned man, relegated to one side, and left to rot in my misery and squalor. If it was now, then it would all be different. I cannot sing the praises of the National Health Service of Great Britain highly enough. It is still a privilege to say that I am British... not in a nationalistic way, but because of the NHS... **a wonderful institution...** much like your present queen, as I admire her more than I can say... and the Commonwealth.

I would like to say 'thank you' to a doctor called Jazz, as I witnessed him help *Skylark,* in her local casualty department. He was a good kind man, who went the extra mile. It was nothing major, but he did what he didn't have to... so, thank you Jazz, for your kindness, from an old monarch who is still proud of his country.

Now, back to George.... I heard rumours of what he was up, to when I was an active king. I thought he was an unfit son, to rule after me. I said as much to my dear wife, who stands with me now; along

160

with another son of mine, who was the Duke of York. If I could have ousted George from the succession, then I think I would have done it. I threatened to and said as much to his face, during a particularly vindictive argument we had. So, no wonder things turned out the way they did!

On one occasion, he made advances to the wife of a courtier. She refused him (you couldn't blame her) so he blocked her and ignored her husband, which resulted in them having no friends and being ostracised. How cruel, but that is how he was... not now though... far from it. I welcomed him with a true father's love, when he died, and I can honestly say that I love him. He is a different man, but that is his story and only he can tell it.

As for me, my life is a lot different; as I am sure you can guess. I love my country still, but in a better way than how I did as king; as I could have been a little proud, priggish, and intolerant. I have learnt my lesson and it is a pity, as I would do a lot of things differently, if given another chance. You only get one opportunity to be monarch; it never comes around again, and I don't need to explain why, as I am sure it is obvious. That is why I am so very, very, proud of your current queen. You have the best, and I only ever want the best for my people, as I still think of you like that... my people of Great Britain... I send greetings to you all.

With the greatest of respect,
George

...FOLLOWED BY THE FOURTH OF THAT NAME

ME, ME, ME
(23/04/18 - 17:16)

I didn't know how selfish I were *[sic]* until I died, and found myself in the arms of love... literally so, as I was guided to my destination by an angelic vibration, who took me to the Halls of Rest. After that it was a little - or I suppose I had better be more accurate - a lot of soul searching, looking at my life and karma. I shouted my head off and told all and sundry that I was a king, and did not want to be treated in such a way. It did me little good, as nobody took any notice... which infuriated me even more!

I was used to shouting and having my every need taken care of. After papa died, and I was king, it got better... except for the queen, I never did like her, so I was glad when I didn't have to suffer her any more. We don't speak, so she is not by my side, and I am sorry, as she was the mother to my only legitimate heir... who doesn't want to know me either... give it time, they said. I have, and nothing much has changed, but that is how it is... the nature of life and freewill.

I am sorry for a lot, and nothing more than for the treatment of papa. I was cruel... I can see it, and have been shown the cruelty I gave to the men and women I felt prevented me from having what I wanted. Good thing I was the oldest, otherwise who knows what I might have got up to. I never had enough - ever - of what I wanted! It's easy for me to say now, but I couldn't for a long time.

When papa said that I behaved in a way that a man and wife were ostracised, it wasn't the first, and, to my shame, not the last time it happened. Quite a few wives obeyed my every demand, much to their shame and disgust. I liked the idea of the husbands knowing that their field had been ploughed, and their wonder what the crop would be. 'Me, me, me' all of the time! I don't how my wives put up with it, or how it would have ended, if I had been on the throne for longer. I was cunning you see, and liked a bit of intrigue. I had a brain inside my head and knew how to use it, but I was bored, so it wasn't put to good use very often.

I have been portrayed on the television, fairly recently in a drama. They only skimmed the surface of what I was like, so a lot has passed history by. I am grateful! Have I painted a despicable picture of a vainglorious king? Maybe I have, but I tell the truth now, so I will begin again with the 'new me.'

Thank you so much papa, for standing by me after I died, and to you mama. You both accepted me as your son, and only showed me love and respect... which was more than I deserved! I am sorry for how I treated you both as regent, and I ask your forgiveness for the lies I told. To my queen I openly say that if it had all been different, would you have been happy? I cannot answer for you, but if I am honest, I think maybe not! I could never have been the man worthy of you, and for that I am sorry. What I have said to the other women in my life, is for them to say, as and when they ever wish to. It was important to me, for the reader to know, that where I should have given love and respect, I never did, and I am sorry.

Love can work wonders if it is allowed to, and it did with me. My life has changed for the better; all down to my papa and mama. I thank you once again for this gift that you have given to me. It showed me that the road isn't always easy, but with you by my side, I can climb every hill and face the challenges in front of me.

George

PERCY THROWER

IT'S A RIOT…
(24/04/18 - 11:42)

…Of colour, I must add. The gardens in spirit are magnificent, and I want to use my letter to talk about mine; along with the aura of the plants, trees, and couple of other subjects.

First of all, I am an old gardener, and I loved it! I used to plant all manner of things, and see how they would get on. I had quite a bad ant problem once, in one of my gardens, but I worked around them and we got along famously. I liked a bit of a challenge, and I used to think that the fairies worked their magic overnight sometimes. I know different now, but it's a similar kind of thing which can happen. It takes longer than you think, but you treat your garden right, and it will give the same respect back. We can all have one… even a window box can work its way into our hearts and uplift. There are always public parks and gardens, if you live in a flat with no balcony, for a pot or two… if it's safe, of course, on both counts. So, we can all do our bit to help nature and uplift ourselves.

Each plant has its own energy, and of course the trees do. They are interlocked and can communicate with each other. If you have a few of them, it's like a grid underneath the ground, and the energy of each tree connects to the other, and on it goes. They bring healing to the soil and air. There we are… a lot are being cut down, which is doing more harm than good, but each one planted is a blessing to you all.

When the trees are in leaf they all draw energy from the Earth, and send it out into the atmosphere, where the clouds and breeze can move it around the world. So, can you see now why it is important for Rose to reincarnate, with the task she has? Each one of us can help the other, but we can also benefit our friends and neighbours, with the gift of nature.

Skylark's small garden is a work in progress and she knows it, but the tree in her front patch likes what's been done, and is giving off this energy. It has a hedge of purple beech to intertwine its roots with. The hedge is only small, as it's the first year of a new one, but already the energy is mingling nicely. Each will benefit the other and the passerby. So, it's a winning situation for everyone.

The lawn at the back is starting to look a lot better, and will improve more, so that in the summer it is not just lots of bare patches or brown ones. Plants have died because the soil is clay, clay, and more clay, and they didn't like it; especially as we had a late, hard frost, which finished them off. Bit by bit, this garden will improve, with the love it has been given.

Skylark also has two spirit plane helpers, whose names are Bergamot and Truffle… and she has glimpsed them from her kitchen window. Bergamot is a nature sprite, and he is learning all about the creation of gardens, in spirit and practically. Truffle is a large brown owl who accompanies Bergamot everywhere, and brings healing, which he channels easily. You all have such helpers for your gardens; unseen by the majority of you, yet working away to help the plants, trees and herbs, if you grow them.

I still have a garden, and work on mine, and I have my helpers. They are two young Iraqi lads, killed in the fighting in their country. I am teaching them all about how to grow food and ornamental gardens. We work each day on the garden, and I teach them as I go along. They are keen, and that's why I asked them to help me. I could see their delight when I showed them my garden. They asked me no end of questions, so I thought, *why not,* and there we are… my garden is blooming down to their enthusiasm.

What amazed them at first was how the flowers lit up when we walked close to them. So, I explained that's what they do in spirit, because our energy energizes them, and creates a bright aura for us to see and feel. They could see the leaves on the trees shining bright, so I said *'they are channelling what our creator gives to us, and that is the universal energy which is with us here and now.'* Crikey, that drew a big response, and a lot of questions about God... I had to say, to ask some of that of their guides… who wanted to help while they worked with me.

There are a lot of flowers and clouds in colours, in spirit, that go beyond the human spectrum. It was a bit difficult at first, but the lads are used to it now, as they are acclimatised to their new life. As we worked sometimes, they would talk about home and the things they witnessed. I was pleased about that; because I knew then they were beginning a new journey, which would give them hope. I think hope is important. We all need it, in its various forms. Whether it is the hope of a new married life or garden, it keeps us moving along the path of life. Nature can also do that; as how many of us have felt troubled and turned to nature to feel comfort? I know I did, and I can tell that *Skylark* has... and a lot of us do... and there we go again on the subject of Rose, as we are ruining what has the potential to give us hope!

Sometimes Isaiah Abbotsbury, in his development circle, will give a nature based meditation. It always amazes people when they see waterfalls, butterflies and all sorts of things like that. We can see just the same in spirit, as I have a variety of butterflies in my garden; some of them are rare, and others as yet unknown to mankind. They flit and flutter about resting on flowers and oregano, and make us smile, while we work side by side.

They are not the only ones to join us, as we have robins with breasts of red, blue, yellow and some speckled, and they are just as tuneful and bright as they are with you. So, you can see that our creator God has thought about a lot to help us. The big difference to the Earth, is that we are so grateful, and will never burn down or hack at trees for profit, because we know their true value and worth.

*****

CARY GRANT

IT'S NOT HOLLYWOOD, BUT I LIKE IT A LOT... IN FACT, I LOVE IT!
(25/04/18 - 16:03)

I agree with Percy about a lot of what he has said. We are consuming and destroying, and doing no good in the process. It's easy for me to say because I live on another plane to all of you, but sometimes I like to visit and go see what I once knew, so I can speak with authority on what I feel is close to my heart.

The cult of being a celebrity has gone ridiculous, and I am glad that I am no longer part of it. It was bad enough when I walked the carpet, but I wouldn't want it now. I am not sure about selfies either, as I think they feed the ego of a few stars too much. I don't blame any that won't do them, because I wouldn't, and I feel that *Skylark* isn't keen either... then again, she doesn't do any form of social platform, so you won't find her on Facebook or Twitter... even if you hunt, she will not be there. Can't say I blame her. No point in even trying, as unless she is forced to, it will never happen. No website either at the moment... however, that one might be brewing in the ethers, for the communicators, and not for her. Some just like their privacy and do not seek their moment of glory, yet wish to give of their heart and soul.

All of the 'names' in spirit do not seek for themselves. It has no value to behave like that and certainly no monetary one, which fuels the cult of celebrity. We have had a few shout, because their status is not recognised. Admiral Lord Nelson was one of those. He doesn't mind me saying, as he will say it himself in another book, but he was aware of his status, and Caligula still is. You can't take it with you if you have it, and it's the same for money, so do the best you can with both... that's what I would do if given the opportunity.

I try my best with my time, to study in the Halls of Learning, or else help in the Halls of Rest. I particularly enjoy the Halls of Rest, because I can see the good I do, when people awake to their new energy. I also go to another area where I work with the less enlightened souls. I

167

don't do it often, but one or two still recognise me. When I do it's always with my guide Joshua, and one of the skilled angelic-type individuals, who are trying to support the grumpy souls under their care. Because I am still known to a few, I can encourage, but you have to know what you are doing, hence the support I have. I am never left alone when in these levels. I wouldn't want to be, because these individuals are experiencing their karma - which is a challenge - and it's not up to me to interfere. If I am asked to help then I always will, but I never go without knowing whom I am attending and what is expected of me. I can refuse, but so far I have not done that, as the ones I speak to are making progress, and allowing the music Matthew channels to the lower levels, to speak to them. This work is only for the souls on the higher levels of spirit, and not levels one, two, or three... which is why I never go along without Joshua.

I have a dog with me at the moment... a lovely little Jack Russell called Spot. He is my constant companion and I love him. He came to spirit abandoned at birth, and I thought he was a lovely little fella. So, I asked for him to be placed with me and we are inseparable. When I reincarnate, it's already been organised that Spot will be part of my life, as I wouldn't want to be without him, and - I think - he me. We can do that if there is an animal we are close to, and it means that on the Earth they have a good home to go to. All in a day's work by the guides who work with the animals, when they pass to spirit.

So long and look after yourselves. As you do, take care of your friends and family, because they are either about to join your soul group, or are already part of it. It's one big happy family in spirit, and we never forget our Earth ones, so take care along life's journey, because you never know who you might meet.

*****

C.S.LEWIS

A LION WITH A GENTLE ROAR
(26/04/18 - 14:48)

I always liked Aslan whenever I added him to a book or two. I didn't start straight away with this being my main focus, as I wanted to delight children and adults alike, and include goodness along with the perils of hellish behaviour; which we sometimes do to each other. Aslan was always there of course, but I worked so that he would be so natural a part of the story, that no-one would hopefully find it strange, to have a kind, talking lion.

God is like that - so very, very kind - not at all like the pantheon of deities of old. He truly never passes judgement, because it is not in his nature to do that. One retired Archbishop of Canterbury wrote about God, being happy to be God. I must say that it is true, because he can be no other, otherwise he would not be the generous figure he is. I use 'he' because that is what I am used to, but God will show himself in the way that is applicable. We do not call him 'God,' as it is only the Earth which does that. Neither do we worship him, as that is another Earth requirement; but we love and respect him and will go out of our way to help, if he asked, and he does the same for us.

I felt very guilty after I died, when I began to see the truth about the Bible, and calling the Old Testament by that name. I feel it is disrespectful to our Jewish brothers and sisters, and I think that *Skylark* might be in agreement, but I cannot speak for her. I also think differently about the power of the cross, because it has been used as a tool of murder... and none more so than when it was the year of the four emperors, and siege of Jerusalem. The arch which depicts Titus' triumph and the Menorah is not truthful, as he was sickened by the crucifixions and murders, by the walls of Jerusalem. He still had to follow his karma after he arrived to the Halls of Rest... and it is a lie about the Menorah too... a bit of Roman spin on a travesty, and persecution of a people who loved their God. The Romans had to be seen as victorious, such was their psyche.

Jesus came to speak to me and told me about *Skylark*. We met in spirit, but she has no awareness of that. I asked Jesus how could I help, and he said that it was a difficult rock to begin to dislodge, because of the power of the early churchmen, a handful of popes, and one or two attendees at the Council of Trent, who met in secret to talk about the parchments they had read, and its impact on the church. Jesus said that a few have known some of the truth over the years, but have said and done nothing... but that one will!

He was also concerned about the people whom truly love God, and call on him in their time of need, and in their prayers for family and the world. He asked me to make sure in my letter to say that, no matter what is said about the scriptures, that God will answer if he is called upon, and that his love is constant. He is the same as he always was and is, but the visible road will soon begin to be different, and *Skylark* mocked. I am not speaking out of turn as she knows this, but will continue anyway, after she has had a rest.

It's not that writing with us all is exhausting, far from it for her, but she has continued through troubled times, and now wishes to rest before she gets going once more. That is important for any to have balance, because then the world will look a different place once the baton is picked up again. The publishing process has to be gone through, but I know a lot about that, and she will be guided and helped. Yet I doubt any agent will want to know, as they didn't wish to publish Matthews's book... so what makes us any different?

God may say a thing or two, but he can't force his word on anyone and neither would Jesus. Jesus told me that my writings helped *Skylark,* and I am grateful to know that in some small way, I could be of service. I will always be of service, if I can help in any way, as Jesus is my inspiration, and his brothers and sisters. They are souls of light and harmony, purity and love... if only you knew the truth of so much. I hope and pray that one day the Earth will spin on a different axis, not one of evil, but of truth, acceptance, and most importantly love.

God bless

HELLO... MY NAME IS AMEN

(27/04/18 - 16:29)

If there were angels, then I would be thought of as one, as my spiritual understanding and energy is on the same level as Jesus. There are no such things as angels, so perhaps I could be considered a soul of messianic experience, along with Raphael and Rose.

We all have the same views on nature, and our understanding of the philosophy of life has been gained over countless lives, on all planes of consciousness. I think it is important for you to know this, because of what I am about to say...

I will reincarnate to help Rose in her work. I will be a lot older than her, so I will be one of the forerunners of what she will focus on. Just as *Skylark* will be mocked, so will I and my friends, but that will not deter us from the task at hand. Our level and understanding is far greater than *Skylark's*, but just as her garden is a work in progress, so is her own personal evolution, along the road of life. It is important that her identity be kept private, because if she is going to be laughed and scoffed at, at least the attacks will not be to her face, so she can work securely and let people think what they will. We shall do everything we can to make sure that this continues for as long as possible, but of course there is freewill of man to consider. Then again if man can keep secrets about the Bible, perhaps we in spirit can have one or two of our own?

I knew Jesus in his incarnation as the son of man, and worked along with him. I was not the only one, as a man called Michah also did, along with a beautiful soul called John. The keeper of the records will need to search and validate John but it can be done, and Michah will be easier to find, as he is already known.

Are there secret church societies? Of course, and I have been to a lot of their meetings, as I find it interesting... and I feed back to my colleagues the relevant information. Nothing they say is private to us, and every meeting is recorded in the Akashic Records; so we can check if we need to, on a subject or decision. It's a bit strange really to keep love, in all its glory, hidden away for the world not to share. A bit beyond me, but then again, I am too evolved to be judge and jury, as karma will take care of that. That's one of the amazing things about it. If we allow ourselves to take vengeance, we are not allowing karma to work its magic, in the way it only knows, which is one of being impartial. We need to give love, but there are times when it has to be tough love, otherwise a kindly soul could be walked on and taken advantage of.

Isaiah Abbotsbury understands this, well and truly. He is a good, kind man; not always understood, yet he is strong and worldly-wise and very, very, positive. His positivity echoes out and brings strength to others. We see this, and it brings joy to our souls. You see, the good each man and woman does is like a light, shining in the darkness; so the nefarious deeds are the opposite, yet are just as visible, through their dimness and lack of colour. So, when God walks the world, he knows what's what, because of the light of the individual.

When *Skylark* works as a medium, this shines out to the higher levels of spirit. It is the same for Isaiah, as his goodness of heart and soul shines out, when he is helping or listening to someone. His wife Tilly loves nature, and we witness this in the light of her soul and generosity of heart. Three individuals with a strong bond… and they know it! It has to be this way, because Isaiah will protect *Skylark* no matter what, and Tilly will do the same.

You will not be able to learn from them, the character or nature of this individual and say 'ah ha I know who it is!' Yet I want to say *'does it matter who this man or woman is?'* *'She' may have been used throughout the book, but this little bird could be male or female… the same as a robin and other little birds.*

The keeper of the records knows and will check, no doubt, because in his shoes, I would! I would want to validate as much as I could, and check Phoebe's prophecies and find how they match. He will also wish to know more about Marcus and Camilla, because there are gaps to be filled. They will be my friend… just be patient! The clues will be given, which help you to see clearer about their lives.

You know about Demetrius already, so that is nothing new and you will recognise my name on a scrap, and that of my brother Michah's. I speak directly to you my friend, because I have been close to you for some time now. You will know me after you have read this, because of the energy of love, which will draw ever nearer to your heart and soul. God will also speak to you, so do not be afraid when he does, as *Skylark* shows no fear and you need fear nothing! What has happened has been like it for years, and sometimes change, when it comes in circumstances like this, is difficult indeed! God will be with you every step of the way. His feet will guide you on the road of enlightenment, and bring joy to your heart.

*****

LEVI

A LITTLE MORE
(28/04/18 - 17:19)

We are near the end now and *Skylark* is exhausted, not through writing but what life has offered her. When I was close to the end of my life, I could barely move, yet had to. I scurried along as fast as I could to avoid another beating... the life of a Jew in Bergen-Belsen Concentration Camp meant nothing, and we could be easily disposed of. So, if the whole of the Jewish faith had been annihilated, who then would the despotic soldiers have cast their eye on... would Adolph Hitler have been satisfied... no he would not! We were just part of the final solution, he had more countries under his watchful eye, to cleanse, and make room for his perfect friends and their families.

I know this because I have been allowed to read a portion of the Akashic Records, concerning Adolf Hitler, for this letter of mine... otherwise, I would not have been given access under any circumstance! It would have made no difference if I was a Jewish historian... the answer would still have been a polite 'no!'

I saw that Adolf Hitler had more ideas that he wished to put into practice, which would have given free reign to his minions. It could not have continued, because of the goodness and decency of the men and women, sickened by what they witnessed, or the stories they heard... men and women of all faiths and nations, including that of Germany and Austria.

Goodness is inside every soul, as it is that part of us which is linked to God, or Hashem. I am beyond a lot now, as I know that my saviour is just that, and is inside my soul. If he can draw near and speak to *Skylark*, a short while ago - which he did - then I, as an orthodox and righteous man, need fear no repercussion, for doing the same with my letter.

I love my faith, and my brothers and sisters of that faith, so very much. I enjoy the Seder meal, with families into whose homes I go on the Earth. I still have distant relatives, and I may occasionally be thought of... only occasionally, as they have lives to live, and did not know me... they are my flesh and blood, and I think of all men on the Earth as such.

I have forgiven the unthinkable acts of the soldiers, who tortured and then finally beat me to death. Not because of the generosity of my heart, or any form of weakness in me, but because of Jesus, Michah, and John... all Jews, and all persecuted for their acts of faith. Jesus may now be thought to be a Christian symbol, but he is mine also (and Judas Iscariot, whose forgiveness knows no bounds). Men of charity and goodness, all of them; whose deaths were planned by the righteous elite of the Second Temple, in Jerusalem.

Jesus was born a Jew and died one. He may have been part of a revolution, a good one, in which love was uppermost, but Caiaphas was not an example of what a high priest should have been. It was his responsibility, and the men and women involved with him, who were solely responsible for what was intended... and that is the murder of righteous men, by crucifixion. The Jews were not, and never were, part of this treachery, so why are we blamed for it? Why do the scriptures portray this? It is because of the jealousy of a man, and then another after him, who wanted to wash the Jews out of this new movement of goodness and love. It was personal, just as it was for Adolf Hitler. Their blinkered vision brought death, and the karma of this followed through to its conclusion (which for Adolf Hitler is still on-going, and will be for a long time).

A simple act of jealousy and ignorance has been part of the destruction of my people throughout history! It has killed millions, and the ripples are being heard in the world as I speak. How long must it continue? We are a people who have the same rights as everyone else, so how long must the Jews be bated and known as 'Christ killers?'

Perhaps as these books unfold, and you begin to read some of the truths which have been kept hidden for so long, a new perspective will be taken. I hope so, and I pray for it to be so, because then I know I will not have died for no reason... other than a lie!

Amen

JUDAS (yes, THAT ONE... but not with the name ISCARIOT)

WHAT'S IN A NAME? A LOT IF IT'S MINE!
(01/05/18 - 15:24)

So, you have heard from my friend Levi, and what an inspiration he is to me and many others! He has forgiven the unthinkable, looked his captors in the eye, and called them 'brother.' I too have done this, to the man who took my legacy and twisted it to suit his purpose... and in the process, making my name a byword for treachery.

It wasn't easy for Levi, and I also found my journey difficult at times. Forgiveness is healing in mind and body, and also for the soul, yet it is not automatically given.... how can it be when hurt and torment have been inflicted? I found understanding why, helped me to - then - face what I did not want to. When Levi spoke to the guards from Bergen-Belsen he asked why? Why did you do the unspeakable to me and my brothers and sisters, time and again? This has been asked more than once by men and women who died under the Third Reich. The - at times - unfathomable why!

A lot of the guards are still in the lower levels, along with their unstable leaders, and some of the soldiers... one of whom is the commandant of Auschwitz. They will remain until they no longer make fun of what they did, or pretend to be sorry. There are also men and women from paramilitary organisations, who keep them company, but have no knowledge of their whereabouts. Our 'solitary' is just that... no sound, unless it is permitted, and quite often, it is the voices of the persecuted penetrating the darkness of their souls.

We are not cruel in spirit... never think that! On the Earth, it is possible to get away with everything, if it is planned carefully. It cannot be done on arrival here, and none are allowed to reincarnate until their soul is shining, with nothing hidden to fester. We allow the persecuted to talk with their captors, and it is not always gentle on the ear. So be it, as that is the karma of cruelty. Place this on the men and women who perpetrated acts of violence, or any kind of deadly action, then you can imagine - I am sure - that Raphael and his team of co-workers are kept quite busy, and none more so than in the last seventy to eighty years.

Yet, the glory of goodness goes beyond what you can imagine, and I am glad to say that it happens more than what is reported in your media. Just this morning, in Damascus, I witnessed a man helping a crying woman, who had lost her son. I looked where I could, along with the man, as the child was feared to be dead under rubble. I am glad to say, that he was found and returned to his mother. I have seen people helped to escape what is thought to be the inescapable, and felt joy when they cried, realising they were free. I have seen so much good, and it does outweigh the bad, but the little things are often missed under the deluge of destruction, murder, and mutilation.

I cannot say too much, as I do not want to burden you with what I have seen. I want to tell you about the goodness and joy that there is in the world, but I have many years in which to do that, before *Skylark* decides it is time to hand over to the next two, who will write the words of spirit, for you to read.

They do not even know it is their karma to do this, and have no skills along the metaphysical path of life, at this moment. So, we have time yet, before *Skylark* pens a letter from spirit, and talks of her experiences, along with Isaiah. There is no fear in death for *Skylark*, because she knows that it is 'life,' and she can be close to family, if she so wishes. I think she may also keep an eye on a little project she will commence, to make sure it runs smoothly and along ethical grounds, with a proud father by her side. That is for you all to find out about, at the correct time… and it will help Rose!

I want to say thank you to a few people before I finally sign off, and leave to return to Syria and her people. *First of all I would like to thank 'Greenpeace'… somebody has to champion nature! Then we have all the oceanographers, biologists and scientists, who take an interest in the sea… thank you for everything, as step by step, it will have an impact on the fish and coral reefs. To the generous men and women who give of their time to help the life of the sea, when the call is given, blessings to you. To the celebrities who give financially; you know who you are, and so do we. Thanks are also given to everyone who does something to help nature and the world… you are blessed far more than you realise!*

I am passionate about nature and the Earth, and I need to be, if I am going to reincarnate to help Rose. I look forward to this life, because I know of its value. Each one of you will reincarnate, no matter what. Some may take longer than others, because they have more to learn first, and their karma will follow… but the Earth path will be walked again and again. The greater the impact Rose has, the better the chance nature has. Rose will build on what Amen will achieve, and what is already being worked on by good men and women, to help the fish, coral reefs, birds and all aspects of nature. We work as a team with love in our hearts, and it is our joy and privilege to be able to do this.

Amen

GOD

SO MUCH FROM SO MANY, WITH MORE TO FOLLOW...
(04/05/18 - 15:48)

I am not here to judge, despite what the scriptures might say, but I am pleased at what has transpired so far, and I hope you enjoy the words transcribed by *Skylark*. It has been a journey indeed for all of us, as we are enthusiastic for the project. It is not the last by a long way, and in the process I have watched what people spoke about. Not because I said not to say certain things, but to enjoy the words of others. Words are important; words contain energy which can uplift or bring harm. A word of a despot can even maim, or bring about the end of the mortal life. Yet, a word can bring love and express love, and that is what I try to do in my life.

I always do the best I can for the person I am with, and if that is a less than enlightened soul, so be it, because I hope to show by example. Sometimes I am spat at in the lower levels, because they do not like what I say. I am not even the most remotely bothered, because I know it is fear based. Fear can make all of us do terrible things. That is what a lot of the terrorist organisations are about, because they feel this power will bring more to them... it will not, and never will, because the word of karma will always exert a greater influence than fear. What is even greater is love... simple as that... because love will never judge or bring harm, unless it is the Earth, as a lot still has to be learnt about it.

All of the communicators had the freewill to say what they wished... not because I gave it to them, but that is the natural state of things. *Skylark* is keen to finish this book, and I do not blame her in any way, because she wishes to enjoy the summer. She also wants to go clothes shopping, as she has no confidence in her previous choices, so wishes for advice. Personal shoppers have been 'Googled', but her guides and family will help, as it is in her karma, for this to be part of her summer.

Karma is never about being rewarded, but about *'what goes around comes around'*, and it can be difficult to buy clothes, if the skin is troubled with psoriasis, and on the feet. Help is always at hand and only needs to be asked, but asked in a way of love and positivity. Whining never helps, and we hear plenty of that in the lower levels. Sometimes I am irritated by it, if I am honest with you all, but I can never show it or say that I am irritated. That would not be righteous or kind of me, so what I do is try to inspire and show by example, and all of my children do the same.

Raphael cannot get angry if he is shouted at or abused, and on the odd occasion even bribed. None of this works, but love always will. Corny it may sound, but love is in all actions and shapes and forms, so who knows what might happen to you one day, that uplifts you and inspires you with joy.

I am so pleased to know that all of the people in the book enjoyed their letter. They are happy with what they said and do not wish to change anything. It, of course, has to be looked at by the agent and the process gone through. *Skylark* knows about the front cover, as her guide Rachel has already shown it to her, so that's off the list. Then there is the painting of Marcus and Camilla. If it does not become part of this book, I am sure, at some stage, it will be seen by you. Money you see has to come into things and the price of the book. We want as many to read it as possible, but if a painting raises the price, then it could put one or two off, and I and the communicators do not want that. So, we shall have to wait and see, but *Skylark* understands.

The next book will not be commenced until *Skylark* says so. It will be about some of the high level souls in heaven, with one or two letters slotted in-between, which all of us hope you will enjoy. One of the communicators, with a letter, will be John Lennon... he is keen as mustard and can't wait... another will be Linda McCartney, with words of love and inspiration. Then a high level communicator, on level seven, is Matthew from the Halls of Music. He will be joined by Diana, also from level seven, and she works in the Akashic Records... so, I hope that is a little to tempt you all.

It was decided to make this the next book, so you get to know a bit more about who's who, and who does what. If Diana or Matthew pops up in a later book, you will have heard of them and their day to day activities. We will not stop at them, as Amos, a Samaritan apostle, will also sing his song, along with the others... so, for now, until we meet again along life's highway, blessings to you all.

*****

A FORETASTE FROM LEVEL SEVEN

AND A WORD OR TWO FROM LINDA
(04/05/18 - 16:47)

The Akashic Records, in the spirit plane, is full of bright, evolved souls, who make sure that all the actions on the Earth are recorded. The facilities have even amazed the most ardent of computer buffs, so to work here you have to know a lot, and be a little bit 'techy,' if I may use that word. I am Diana, a highly-evolved soul, with a messianic understanding, similar to Amen and Raphael. I look forward to speaking to you all again, and hope that you feel the same enthusiasm as we all do, about the writings which have been thought about and planned for a long time. I will hand over briefly to Linda McCartney, to say just one or two words, to someone who will understand exactly what she means.

*****

I heard the words of love, you said... they are inscribed on my heart, and I feel the same. It is your life and always will be, so live it with joy in your heart, because I do. My life is a wonder, and one day I hope to tell you about it, so until then 'seize the day' and make the most of it, because each one will bring another, and who knows what that holds.

My love to you all,
Linda

Working on this book has been a journey, from the first draft to what you see before you. The experiences have been varied: from laughing out loud at Anne of Cleves' letter (first draft), to crying at the end of Levi's, and thinking what an amazing man he is.

The process has also given me food for thought, with regard to God. I hope it does the same for you, because then you too will wish to know more of the man the Earth has called 'God.'

*Before I sign off, I would like to say to all who **choose** to read this book, that I hope you find joy in its pages. May you feel comfort in the words spoken by the communicators, if they are close to you in heart and soul, and that it illuminates the path you walk.*

Until we meet again, with the very best of wishes,

Skylark

EDITOR'S NOTE

This has been, without doubt, the hardest book I've had to edit, for various reasons. Firstly, *Skylark* receives these letters via dictation*, with very little punctuation, and secondly, considering the nature of the communications, we, respectfully, didn't feel that the language should be changed, unless it was absolutely necessary. *'Who am I to edit the word of God, (et al)?'*

I've always been spiritual myself, and have, in fact, met *Skylark* a few times while travelling my own 'pathway.' I've felt throughout this edit that 'I wasn't working alone,' and *Skylark* wasn't at all surprised when I mentioned this.

I hope all concerned with the production of this book are happy with my work. It has truly been an honour to have been involved, and I have thoroughly enjoyed reading the letters myself.

* *The dictation is of a spiritual nature, and some may think of it as 'automatic writing.' It is given on a clairsentient link, with no punctuation, as the focus for the communicator is the word on the page (apart from once, when God gave a full stop). It is the role of the earth plane editor to perform the given task, working intuitively, aided by their own guide.*

CONTENTS

Lightning Source UK Ltd.
Milton Keynes UK
UKHW021604190220
358984UK00015B/1038

9 781908 760395